LECTURE NOTES ON
PSYCHIATRY

LECTURE NOTES ON
PSYCHIATRY

James Willis
MB, FRCP(Edin), FRCPsych, DPM
Head, Division of Psychiatry
Deputy Medical Director—Operations
King Faisal Specialist Hospital
and Research Centre
Riyadh, Saudi Arabia
Formerly Consultant/Psychiatrist
Guy's Hospital, London
Kings College Hospital,
London, England
and Bexley Hospital
Kent, England

SIXTH EDITION

BLACKWELL

SCIENTIFIC PUBLICATIONS

OXFORD LONDON EDINBURGH

BOSTON MELBOURNE

© 1964, 1968, 1972, 1974, 1979,
1984 by Blackwell Scientific
Publications Editorial offices:
Osney Mead, Oxford, OX2 0EL
8 John Street, London, WC1N 2ES
9 Forrest Road, Edinburgh,
   EH1 2QH
52 Beacon Street, Boston
   Massachusetts 02108, USA
99 Barry Street, Carlton
   Victoria 3053, Australia

First published 1964
Reprinted 1966
Second Edition 1968
Reprinted 1970
Third Edition 1972
Fourth Edition 1974
Reprinted 1976
Fifth Edition 1979
Portuguese Edition 1980
Sixth Edition 1984

Photoset by Enset Ltd
Midsomer Norton, Bath, Avon
Printed and bound in Great Britain by
Billings & Sons Limited,
Worcester.

DISTRIBUTORS

USA
   Blackwell Mosby Book Distributors
   11830 Westline Industrial Drive
   St Louis, Missouri 63141

Canada
   Blackwell Mosby Book Distributors
   120 Melford Drive, Scarborough
   Ontario, M1B 2X4

Australia
   Blackwell Scientific Book
   Distributors
   31 Advantage Road, Highett
   Victoria 3190

British Library
Cataloguing in Publication Data

Willis, James
   Lecture notes on psychiatry.—6th ed.
   1. Mental illness
   I. Title
   616.89   RC454

ISBN 0-632-01174-2

CONTENTS

ACKNOWLEDGEMENTS

Acknowledgements to 1st Edition

This book could not have been written without the encouragement of many former teachers and colleagues. Dr David Stafford-Clark was chief among these. Dr Colin McEvedy gave much valuable advice and Miss D. Harlow typed the manuscripts. The publishers, Mr Per Saugman particularly, have been extremely patient throughout and for this I am most grateful.

Acknowledgements to 2nd Edition

I should like to express my gratitude to Professor Jack Tizard and Dr Ronald MacKeith for their advice on the re-written chapter on Subnormality. Also Dr Stephen MacKeith for his perceptive comments and helpful criticism.

Acknowledgements to 6th Edition

The 6th edition involved a considerable amount of rewriting and revision and for their assistance in this, I am grateful to Mesdames Vilma Contreras, Lourdes Corpus, Yvonne Lock and Maria Lourdes P. Martinez and also to my friends and colleagues at the King Faisal Specialist Hospital and Research Centre for their continued encouragement.

AN INTRODUCTION TO
PSYCHIATRY

Medical students often say that they find psychiatry interesting but disappointing. Interesting because psychiatry is a clinical subject and all students seem to like this, disappointing because, as they frequently put it, 'it all seems vague and woolly'; also they are put off by the apparent lack of a sound body of psychiatric knowledge and the disagreements about diagnosis and treatment.

This book is not intended as a comprehensive text, the length and omissions should make that clear. It is written to try and answer the sort of questions that students seem to need answering fairly quickly when they start a psychiatric clerkship. They find themselves in difficulties because they have to learn a new language and acquire a new set of concepts of illness, if they are to retain any interest in psychiatry at all. Too often they are discouraged from trying and emerge as doctors with blind spots for psychological illness.

The training of medical students remains a subject for discussion, research and revision but as yet it does not adequately prepare the majority of students for much more than a somewhat unwary first encounter with the practice of psychiatry. Students tend to have heard that psychiatry is a discipline 'by schisms rent asunder' and this may make them unnecessarily sceptical, particularly if their half notions are reinforced by the misinformation still so freely available from an intriguing range of sources.

Also there *are* unresolved dilemmas about what things should be taught. Certain medical schools may favour a clinical approach based on traditional diagnosis, treatment and prognosis. Others favour early introduction of the student to psychological principles—showing him how human behaviour may be governed by unconscious processes and relating this to interpersonal relationships and *their* consequences in people's life styles and behaviour. Whilst others have suggested that students need to be introduced quite early to the practice of psychotherapy—since this will provide them with a living illustration of human psychopathology. But while these divisions of opinions may exist (since

vii

as yet no one has *proved* what are the needs of students), at least we see
the beginnings of a medical student training in which the importance is
stressed of the patient as an individual and as a social being—not a mere
collection of mechanical systems.

Medical student training may be the subject of discussion, research
and revision, but the fact is that it does not equip students for the easy
assimilation of psychiatric attitudes and ideas.

For a start the student finds that he needs to re-examine his own
concept of disease. Up to now he has had no difficulty in seeing that
patients with tumours, fractures, diabetes etc., are in diseased states.
His psychiatric patient, on the other hand often appears well and
disclaims symptoms; no handicap is obvious until he finds that the
patient's inner life is dominated by a series of fantastic beliefs which
have caused him to alter his way of living so that he is now in hospital—
maybe against his will. What does he make of that? Is he ill? Are there
many patients like that and if so what is wrong with them?

Psychiatry deals with this sort of patient and many others; what they
all have in common is disturbances affecting their behaviour, emotions,
thinking and perception. Perhaps most important of all is the recognition that 'psychiatric illness' occurs when these disturbances are real
changes which persist and exceed commonly accepted limits of
normality and are changes about which the patient may complain, be
bothered and puzzled about—so that we are justified in regarding them
as symptoms. This is the psychiatric frame of reference. We can set it
down more formally by saying that we recognize psychiatric illness by
examining the patient's

1   behaviour,
2   mood,
3   perception,
4   thought content,
5   intelligence level,
6   memory,   } cognitive functions
7   concentration,
8   orientation in space and time,

and by discerning abnormalities make a clinical diagnosis.

The manifestations of psychiatric disorder can be recognized without
great difficulty. The medical student's difficulty in examining
psychiatric patients can be traced to:

1   lack of method, and
2   lack of practice.

It is our intention in this work to provide a simple clinical guide to psychiatric language and syndromes.

The student should always remember
1   to listen carefully,
2   to record conscientiously,
3   to avoid interpreting and speculating about what he supposes the patient means,
4   to get a history from as many informants as possible,
5   only to use words that he understands.

Classification of mental illness

The ideal classification would be based on aetiology. In psychiatry this is rarely possible except in certain organic disorders (e.g. G.P.I., delirium tremens), so that classification tends to be descriptive, that is to say based on the dominant observable features of the syndrome (e.g. anxiety, depression). This is unsatisfactory but inevitable at present. The danger of the descriptive method lies in the possibility that the name given to a syndrome may assign to it a separate existence. For example we may talk about schizophrenia without assuming that there is a 'thing' schizophrenia. If the word is allowed to assume a concrete reality this stifles further enquiry.

Classification then may be unsatisfactory but necessary since we have to achieve some sort of order. Many systems are used, some are more satisfactory than others. In this work we will use this classification: it is clinical, oversimple no doubt, but adequate.
1   Affective disorders
      Depressive states
      Unipolar and bipolar affective disorder
2   Schizophrenia
      Simple
      Hebephrenic
      Catatonic
      Paranoid
3   Organic syndromes
      Delirium and subacute delirium
      Dementia
4   Neuroses
      Anxiety
      Hysteria

CHAPTER 1
THE HISTORY—
SOME TERMS DEFINED—
THE EXAMINATION

The psychiatric history, like any other is an attempt to set down an accurate account of an illness. It is taken in the usual way but the technique should be modified to permit the patient to tell his story without becoming unnecessarily distressed. Distress and misery are commonplace since so often the history refers to painful topics. The patient should be allowed to start off wherever he likes in the history rather than adhering to a rigid scheme of questioning—there should be time to sort out all the data afterwards.

THE FIRST INTERVIEW

One should attempt to take as full a history as possible on this occasion but it may not be a practical, nor a humane possibility. This first interview is likely to be an event of great significance for the patient—he may have been dreading it or preparing himself for it for days and when it is over it is something he is likely to remember. With this in mind the doctor should do all he can to make the experience bearable for the patient and resist the temptation to question like a cross-examining attorney.

How to elicit a history

Students often complain that they don't know what questions to ask the patient and are surprised when a more skilled examiner unearths facts they had missed. The answer to this difficulty is relatively simple. A history, after all, is only an edited series of answers to an elaborate and unstructured questionnaire and with practice the expert learns what questions to ask, and constructs his own questionnaire. Listening to others taking a history illustrates this very well—actually this is as good a way of learning to take a history as any, and not widely enough used.

1

Symptoms and signs

Modes of presentation and symptomatology are of a different order in psychiatry, though not inevitably so. One patient complains of bodily symptoms, another brings a story of persecution by others, whilst another complains of altered mood and poor concentration. Many patients have no complaint at all and deny all symptoms, the history being given by relatives who tell a different story.

The relationship

The relationship between doctor and patient starts as the patient comes through the door. The patient's initial greeting may be friendly, hostile, suspicious or just neutral. Whatever it is, the doctor stands to lose or gain a great deal by his own behaviour. There is no substitute for *friendly politeness* and no place for patronizing pseudo-omniscience. The patient should be accepted as he is and not subjected to value judgements. The talkative patient should be permitted to tell his story as he likes at first, and then be guided through the areas that the doctor wants to cover so that a comprehensive history can be taken. The reticent patient needs encouragement, and although this can be difficult, one must not put words in the patient's mouth.

THE PLACE OF HISTORY TAKING IN DIAGNOSIS

There is a fashionable tendency for some psychiatrists to decry diagnosis, to question the 'medical model' of psychiatric illness. And there is good sense in many such criticisms. Just because a person consults a psychiatrist this does not automatically confer on him the status of being ill. This needs to be mentioned, for some psychiatrists talk as if they believed that this were the case! Practical psychiatry should remain a clinical subject in which traditional medical training in diagnosis etc. are of clear usefulness without being overvalued. The clinical approach remains, to date, a humane and pragmatic one. We should recognize too that the clinician has always to be aware of how it is that individual, psychological and social forces may influence the content of an illness but not the form of clinical syndromes—and form is what diagnosis is about. Perhaps we would do well always to remember the large gaps in our knowledge and resist the temptation to conceal them with all embracing theories which illuminate all and clarify nothing save their continued existence as untested and untestable hypotheses— ugly white elephants which retain our mistakes long after we have forgotten them.

Diagnosis is made by examination of the mental state. The history contributes to our understanding of the mental state—it is a pointer to the diagnosis. History taking takes time. One cannot learn much about a patient in 5 minutes or even 50, for that matter. There is no place in good psychiatry or good medical practice for the 'spot diagnosis'—in psychiatry it generally turns out to be no diagnosis at all. Most diagnostic errors can be traced to poor history taking.

A scheme for history taking

A formal scheme has to be used for writing down the history. This does not mean that one has to take it down in the following order.

Complaint

This should consist merely of a short statement of the patient's complaint, or if he has none, a short statement of the reason for his referral for psychiatric opinion.

Family history

In this, one should enumerate the *parents* and *siblings,* noting carefully such details as *ages, employment, illnesses, causes of death.* It should also include where possible some account of the incidence of any *familial psychiatric illnesses.* Direct questions should always be asked about incidence in the family of epilepsy, delinquency, alcoholism and drug use, and suicide and attempted suicide. The family history too should give some information about the *social status* and *inter personal relationships* within the family.

Personal history

This should commence with a note of the date and place of birth. Any information available about the patient's infant development should be recorded with particular reference to *health* during childhood, *neurotic symptoms* and *infant milestones. School record* should next be noted down, concentrating not only on the names of the schools and the leaving age etc., but attempting if possible to state the individual's attainments at school and to estimate his social popularity etc. *Occupations* should next be considered in chronological order with wages earned and status. These details may throw some light on the person's pre-morbid personality and also on the evolution of the illness since frequently work performance is impaired by psychiatric illness—it may be the presenting complaint, e.g. 'can't seem to cope with my job ... keep having to change my job ... can't settle to anything'. It is also useful to make some note of the individual's relationships with employers and colleagues.

Menstrual and psycho-sexual history

This includes the usual menstrual history with the addition of psycho-sexual topics such as how the patient acquired sexual information, his/her *varieties* and *frequency of sexual practice* and *fantasy*. The marital history should be noted with details of *engagement, marriage* and *pregnancies* and their outcome. There should always be careful enquiry about psychiatric disturbance during and after pregnancy.

Past illnesses

Recorded chronologically. With details of any admissions and treatments received.

Past psychiatric illnesses

Recorded chronologically.

Pre-morbid personality

An attempt should be made to describe as accurately as possible the individual's personality before the illness. This is the part of the history that usually causes the great difficulty since our methods of describing the personality are so imperfect. In practice, the most helpful descriptions of the pre-morbid personality are not those which consist merely of one or two adjectives but rather those which give a portrait of the individual, consisting of a few paragraphs.

Description of present illness

This should be a detailed chronological account of the illness from the onset to the present time. There should always be an accurate description of the order, mode and speed of the change in the person's symptomatology.

THE PSYCHIATRIC EXAMINATION

The examination of the patient does not stop short at the examination of his mental state but includes a general physical examination, and where needed, physical investigation. Many individuals referred to a psychiatrist turn out to have either associated physical disease or else disease causing their altered mental state. Examples of the latter would be such conditions as cerebral tumours, general paresis, disseminated sclerosis and myxoedema. The physical examination, too, has a positive value in the reassurance of a hypochondriacal patient.

PSYCHIATRIC LANGUAGE—A FEW TERMS DEFINED

Before going any further into details of how we examine and describe the mental state, here is a list of commonly used psychiatric terms.

Anxiety
A feeling of fear or apprehension commonly accompanied by autonomic disturbance. Anxiety may be felt by healthy subjects in the face of stress such as examinations etc., but is described as morbid anxiety when it pervades the mental life of an individual.

Depression
Pathological mood disturbance resembling sadness or grief. Depression is described as reactive when it can be related to an apparent causal agent, and endogenous when it appears out of the blue. The mood change is accompanied by characteristic disturbance of sleep, energy and thinking.

Dementia
Progressive, irreversible intellectual impairment. Dementia is caused by organic brain disease.

Delirium
An organic mental state in which altered consciousness is combined with psychomotor overactivity, hallucinosis and disorientation.

Depersonalization
A subjective feeling of altered reality of the self, e.g. 'I'm not myself any more. I feel as if I were dead; I feel unreal. Different to what I was. If only I could wake up.'

Derealization
A subjective feeling of altered reality of the environment, e.g. 'Everything around me seems strange like in a dream. Things don't look or feel the same,' usually associated with depersonalization.

Delusion
A false belief which is inappropriate to an individual's socio-cultural background and which is held in the face of logical argument. True delusions commonly have a paranoid colouring (q.v.) and are held with extraordinary conviction. Delusion is thus a primary and fundamental experience in which incorrect judgements are made. The experience of delusion proper precedes its expression in words and hence, when stated, is incomprehensible and beyond argument, e.g. 'I was walking along the street and saw a dog and immediately I knew by the way it stood that I was a special person predestined to save mankind.'

Delusional ideas
Delusional ideas differ from true or primary delusions in that instead of arising out of the blue they occur against a background of disturbed mood and are entirely explicable in that context. Thus the severe delusional ideas of guilt and condemnation and persecution shown by a psychotic depressive are seen to be an outgrowth of the depressive state. In the same way the delusional notions of grandeur and exaltation of the manic spring from his elevated mood—a mood which brings with it breezy overconfidence and insouciance which can easily develop into ideas of omnipotence.

Flight of ideas
Accelerated thinking, characteristically seen in hypomanic and manic illness. The association between ideas are casual, and are determined by such things as puns and rhymes. However links are detectable and the flight can be followed.

Hallucinations

A perception occurring in the absence of an outside stimulus (e.g. hearing a voice outside one). Hallucinations are particularly common in schizophrenia. Patients hear voices which tell them to do things, comment on their actions, utter obscenities or murmur wordlessly. The phenomenon of 'hearing one's thoughts spoken aloud' is encountered in schizophrenia. Hallucinations are described as hynagogic if they are experienced whilst falling asleep and hypnopompic if experienced whilst waking up.

Hypochondriasis

Preoccupation with fancied illness. Hypochondriacal features are common in depression and may be found as bizarre phenomena in schizophrenia. Hypochondriasis may be the central feature of a hysterical illness. It seems likely that hypochondriasis does not exist on its own but is usually a manifestation of some underlying psychiatric condition or personality disorder.

Illusion

A perceptual error or misinterpretation. These commonly occur in organic mental states, particularly delirium. A patient in such a state misinterpreted a building outside his window as being a liner about to sail.

Ideas of reference

The patient who has ideas of reference experiences events and perceives objects in his environment as having a special significance for himself. For example a patient noticed that all the TV programmes she saw indicated to her in some unusual way that she had been singled out for observation by a secret police force.

Neurosis and psychosis

Although widely used the terms lack precise definition and give rise to disagreement. A working definition would be that neurotic illnesses are states in which anxiety, mild mood change and preservation of contact with reality are the rule. The neurotic patient is only too aware of his illness, and never loses contact with reality. In psychotic states, the patient loses contact with reality, there is a tendency towards the more bizarre manifestations of psychiatric disturbance as a common finding. Mood change when present is likely to be profound.

Thus it appears that we base our definitions of neurosis and psychosis on severity of symptoms rather than anything else. Such an unsatisfactory state of affairs must persist until more is known about the aetiology of psychiatric disorders in general.

Mannerism

A habitual expressive movement of the face or body. Normal mannerisms are appropriate but pathological mannerisms are inappropriate (e.g. in schizophrenia).

Obsessional phenomena (obsessive compulsive phenomena)

These are contents of consciousness of an unpleasant and recurrent sort which the patient experiences but which he resists. These contents may include words, ideas, phrases and acts. This is well exemplified by a patient who had to perform every act of washing, dressing and eating nine times or else he became anxious and distressed.

Paranoid

This is a widely known psychiatric term and about as widely misused. It derives from the Greek *para nous*, i.e. beyond reason. It has been used for years to describe 'classic' signs of psychosis—particularly those that encompass delusions of grandeur or those of a fantastic sort.

Recent use of the term has tended to assign to it the meaning of 'persecutory', thus paranoid delusions become delusions of persecution and suspicion, oversensitive people are regarded as 'paranoid'. This is no doubt related to the fact that ideas of persecution *are* commonplace in psychosis so that by a process of condensation paranoid = psychotic = persecuted. But this is an incorrect way of using the term which should be reserved for the formal description of delusions and syndromes characterized by 'persecution, grandeur, litigation, jealousy, love, envy, hate, honour, or the supernatural' (Lewis 1970).

The term may be extended to describe the mechanism of projection by which a person refers events, even trifles, to himself, but it should be emphasized that the term implies a mechanism of psychotic intensity and not the sensitive ideas and feelings which are part of the normal experience of many.

Passivity feeling

A feeling of bodily influence or control by outside agents. This phenomenon is commonly found in schizophrenia.

Schizophrenia
A syndrome, occurring mainly in young people, in which are found characteristic disturbances of *thinking, perception, emotion* and *behaviour.* The illness tends to lead to disintegration of the personality.

Schizophrenic thought disorder
A characteristic type of disturbance of thinking, found only in schizophrenia, in which there is a basic disturbance of the process of conceptual thinking. This shows itself in the patient's speech, which reflects his impaired logical thinking. Early schizophrenic thought disorder often manifests itself as a subjective difficulty in thinking clearly. In its most severe form thought disorder reduces patients' talk to fragmented nonsense—'word salad'. Certain German psychiatrists have stressed the clinical importance of the description by a patient of the experience of feeling that thoughts are inserted into the head, or that they are being withdrawn from the head, or that one's thoughts are being spoken aloud outside of one (Gedankenlauten werden). Such manifestations are usually regarded as being of prime importance in making the diagnosis of schizophrenia.

GENERAL ADVICE REGARDING THE EXAMINATION OF AND DESCRIPTION OF THE MENTAL STATE

The signs of mental disturbance can be elicited provided one learns how to do this, in much the same way that one learns to elicit physical signs in general medicine. However, one should avoid leading questions, and also it is important to avoid making remarks or comments to the patient which may implant in his mind disruptive or disturbing ideas. In this way one can avoid *interpreting* to the patient the *apparent meaning* of his experiences or feelings. Interpretation should be avoided and left to the expert. The patient should not be antagonized if he appears to be uncooperative. Antagonism, resistance and evasiveness can usually be overcome by handling the situation in a non-commital way. Recording the patient's talk verbatim is extremely useful but may antagonize a prickly patient. Here is a scheme for the mental state:

Behaviour

In describing the patient's behaviour one should try as far as possible to get an accurate description of how the patient behaves during interview. One starts by observing the patient's behaviour, instead of just taking it for granted. Points to note include:

1 the patient's general level of consciousness;
2 awareness of what is going on around him;
3 his level of cooperation with the examiner;
4 whether he is able to make contact with the examiner at interview;
5 the patient's predominant facial expressions and whether they are appropriate;
6 his use of gesture;
7 activity—free or constrained, continuous or interrupted;
8 the presence of agitation;
9 use of mannerisms.

This is not a complete list but is only intended as a guide.

Talk

It is usual to consider both the *form* and the *content* of the patient's talk. The *form* is the manner of talk, i.e. how it presents, sustained, interrupted, fast or slow etc. The simplest way to examine the content of the patient's talk is by making a verbatim sample. Content means the predominant topics.

Mood

Here we try to comment on whether the patient's mood is sustained or variable. What is the predominant mood as far as possible? Quite often a description of the patient's mood cannot be put down in one word, e.g. depressed. A useful way of enquiring about the patient's mood is to ask some questions such as 'How do you feel in yourself'? or 'How are your spirits?'

Thought content

Delusions

These can only be elicited by careful questioning. Some patients will talk very spontaneously about their delusions and express a wide variety of illogical ideas. Other patients will need to be questioned. Paranoid delusions are often persecutory and to elicit them requires bland questions which do not arouse the patient's suspicions too strongly. Such questions are 'Are people treating you as they should?' or 'How are people behaving towards you, do you suppose?' are often quite useful. Enquire about the patient's attitude to his own self. Ask whether he feels he has changed in any way, or whether he feels he is a good or bad person. This may help to elicit feelings of guilt and self-recrimination.

Hypochondriacal ideas

It is important to recognize that hypochondriacal concern is an extremely common finding amongst psychiatric patients. Thus the anxious patient may have a considerable amount of hypochondriacal fears surrounding bodily symptoms of anxiety such as palpitations etc. On the other hand the severely depressed patient may present with severe hypochondriasis which may well be missed by the examining doctor until he is aware of the significance of hypochondriasis in depression (q.v.). Bizarre hypochondriacal notions tend to be found in schizophrenic illnesses.

Obsessive compulsive phenomena

Here one should enquire about habits surrounding various aspects of the patient's daily life. For instance the patient with an obsessional disorder may have rituals concerned with washing and eating etc. which he feels obliged to carry out, and which occasion him much discomfiture. Very often the patient will be extremely ashamed of this type of symptom and discuss it only with difficulty.

Perceptual disturbance

Here one records hallucinations and illusions, noting the modality of the hallucination and its content. Also the occasions on which they tend to occur.

Cognitive testing

Memory

The patient's account of his history when compared with other informants will give some assessment of his memory for past events.

Recent memory may be adequately tested by asking the patient to give an account of the preceding 24 hours. The ability to retain new information and reproduce it may be tested as follows:

1   Give the patient a name, address and telephone number. Ask him to repeat it immediately and to reproduce it in 5 minutes.

2   Ask the patient to listen to the Babcock sentence and repeat it, e.g. 'One thing a Nation must have to become rich and great is an adequate secure supply of wood.'

Orientation

Record the patient's account of the time of day, date and place.

Concentration

One should record the patient's level of attention to the questions asked him and also try and test his concentrating ability by asking him to subtract 7 from 100 until he can go no further, noting the number of mistakes and the time taken.

General information and intelligence

Under the heading 'General Information' one attempts to assess the individual's store of general knowledge. Useful questions here will include such things as the patient's familiarity with current affairs, topics of the day and familiarity with reigning figures and political names. Intelligence can be assessed quite roughly clinically bearing in mind the patient's educational background and professional attainments and some attempt should be made to place a patient on the scale:

1   below average;

2   average;

3   superior.

Insight

Assessing the patient's insight is the most difficult thing of all. It does not merely mean asking the patient whether he knows whether he is ill or not although of course awareness of the existence of illness is an important criterion of insight. But in deciding and commenting upon the patient's level of insight, one wants to know too, how aware the patient is of the extent of his illness and its effect on other people, such as his family, employers, colleagues, etc. One wants to know too, whether the patient has any idea of how his illness seems to others or how he might feel about a similar illness in other people. Some idea about his insight might be gleaned from his views regarding future plans and so on.

Special investigations

Special investigations of the mental state include the use of tests of psychological function. It is important to point out that there is no 'ideal' psychological test—a fact which surprises some students whose notions of clinical psychology are likely to be hazy. It is less than fair to clinical psychology to suppose that this is a professional discipline devoted to 'testing' psychiatric patients though psychological investigation, properly used, is used to clarify problems in diagnosis and to guide, assess and plan treatment and rehabilitation. The sophisticated use of psychological *testing* relies on the use of batteries of tests and careful selection of testing procedures by the psychologist and *not* by the doctor.

Common areas of psychiatric scrutiny include the measurement of intelligence and assessment of personality structure.

Frequently used intelligence tests include the Raven Progressive Matrices and the Mill Hill Vocabulary Scale. These are tests of general and verbal ability, are well standardized, relatively simple to administer either to individuals or groups, and give an acceptable assessment of the intelligence level. The Wechsler Adult Intelligence Scale (W.A.I.S.) is another well standardized intelligence test which is more comprehensive than the former. It includes tests of performance as well as verbal tests. Personality assessment relies first of all on the use of projective tests which are thought to reveal the subject's unconscious process, e.g. the subject is asked to describe what he sees in a pattern of ink blots (Rorschach) or to make up a story about an ambiguous picture (Thematic Apperception Test).

Other methods of personality assessment include questionnaires which are designed to identify patterns of personality structure. An example of this is the Minnesota Multiphasic Personality Inventory (M.M.P.I.). This questionnaire consists of over 500 items. The questions are designed in such a way as to tap attitudes in the respondent which may be construed as indicating in the personality the presence of elements going to make up a particular personality structure and also to reveal the presence of elements resembling at least certain clinical psychiatric syndromes.

Laboratory investigations

There are no routine investigations in psychiatric practice although chest X-ray, skull X-ray and syphilitic serology still remain the basic and important investigations that every patient should have apart from a complete blood picture and urine analysis.

The advent of *computerized tomography* has made available one of the most revolutionary investigations in the exclusion of organic brain disease. And although no one would regard this as a routine investigation in psychiatric practice, it is beyond question that it will be a frequently used investigation.

A good rule is that the doctor should always have some good reason for using a special investigation rather than resorting to whole batteries of special tests.

Finally the essentials of this history and mental state should be summarized in a formulation of the patient's illness, presenting a bird's eye view of the diagnosis, likely treatment and possible prognosis.

REFERENCES

Hare E. H. (1973) A short note on pseudo-hallucinations. *Br. J. Psychiat.*, 122, 469.

Jaspers K. (1968) *General Psychopathology* (Translated from 7th edn by J. Hoenig and M. W. Hamilton). Manchester University Press, Manchester.

Kendall R. E. (1973) Psychiatric diagnoses. A study of how they are made. *Br. J. Psychiat.*, 122, 437.

Laing R. D. (1982) *The Voice of Experience: Experience Science and Psychiatry.* Allen Lane, London.

Lewis A. J. (1970) Paranoia and paranoid: a historical perspective. *Psychol. Med.*, 1, 2.

Mayer Gross W., Slater E. & Roth M. (1960) In *Clinical Psychiatry.* Cassell, London.

Stengel E. (1959) Classification of mental diseases. *Bull W.H.O.*, 21, 601.

Stevenson I. (1959) The Psychiatric Interview. In *American Handbook of Psychiatry*, vol. 1, 197. Basic Books, New York.

CHAPTER 2
AFFECTIVE DISORDERS

Introduction

The affective disorders are all characterized by a primary disturbance of mood, the polar extremes of which range from profound sadness and dejection in severe depression to the breezy insightless hilarity of mania. Less severe varieties of mood disturbance may be seen in so-called neurotic depression and lead to a surprising degree of handicap. The common thread that unites all these disorders is mood disturbance, which is only recognized as a manifestation of illness when it is excessive and goes beyond the customary fluctuations of mood that are part of the fabric of ordinary mental life. In affective disorder, however, mood disturbance is not merely extreme, it is also disproportionate. Another important aspect of pathological mood change is that it is unresponsive to outside influence—the depressed patient is not easily reassured nor cheered up any more than is the hypomanic patient even slightly put off by comments on his exuberant behaviour. Any other manifestations occurring in affective disorder, whether they be physiologic or perceptual, are secondary and follow in the wake of the primary mood change.

CLASSIFICATION OF AFFECTIVE DISORDER

Kraepelin was the first to describe manic depressive insanity, i.e. a disorder in which excitement and depression alternated. After Kraepelin, physicians looked beyond manic depressive disorders and became more aware of depression as a disorder on it own.

Depressions are often described either as being *reactive* or *endogenous*. Since these terms are in such common use some explanation must be made of them, but it is a fact that their use is controversial.

Reactive depression is usually so named if the depression can be shown to satisfy the following conditions: (a) Its onset follows some obvious cause in the patient's life, such as loss of a job, broken engagement, examination failure, etc. (b) The content of the illness is concerned with

15

the cause to the exclusion of everything else. (c) The illness would not have come on if the precipitating event had not occurred. Many people prefer to use the term neurotic depression rather than reactive depression.

Endogenous depression is so named if: (a) The depression arises out of the blue, unrelated to external events. (b) There is diurnal variation of mood. (c) There is sleep disturbance with early morning waking.

In practice the distinction between these two 'types' of depression is hard to make—what at first sight appears to be 'reactive' depression then turns out to be 'endogenous' by virtue of the presence of diurnal mood variation, early waking, etc.

Current practice in the classification of depressions still reflects a division of opinion. In addition to the reactive (neurotic)-endogenous dichotomy of depression, other people have preferred to classify depressions as primary or secondary. A primary depressive state is one which arises apparently spontaneously and is not related to any preceding physical or psychiatric illness or unfavourable life event.

Finally it is now recognized that there are differences between these two types of severe affective disorder. Manic depressive illness or bipolar affective disorder being distinguished from unipolar disorder, which is always depressive in type and shows a different genetic inheritance, response to treatment and possibly a different biological basis.

DEPRESSION

In depression the mood resembles sadness or grief but is sustained, unlike the transitory mood changes that many people experience in response to various stresses or from one part of the day to the other. The important thing about depressive states is that this change of mood is sustained and that it exceeds quantitatively and qualitatively these ordinary variations. In addition, there are other bodily and emotional disturbances. There is no point in expanding the concept of depression in an attempt to explain away every variety of human unhappiness.

It is often hard to distinguish 'true' depression from states of unhappy malaise that trouble people with abnormal personalities, those who abuse drugs or alcohol or, for that matter, people with chronic painful illnesses. These are more than unhappiness, yet they are not depression—often they are referred to as states of 'dysphoria'.

The accompaniments of depression are:

1 insomnia;
2 loss of energy;
3 loss of interest;
4 anorexia;
5 weight loss;
6 decreased libido and impotence.

Aetiology

Incidence and prevalence

Depression is a common disorder. General practice consultation rates have been calculated at 31 per 1 000 for neurotic depression—population surveys suggest even higher rates up to 15%.

Bipolar affective disorder and mania are rarer disorders with incidence rates of 0.6 and 0.02% in the general population respectively.

Heredity

Early attempts at identifying a genetic factor looked for genetic differences between endogenous and neurotic depression—but so much overlap was found as to render this idea untenable. Leonhard (1959) pointed out that a better dichotomy might be provided by separating affective disorders into bipolar (manic depressive) and unipolar (pure depression) and look for evidence of genetic inheritance in these. Since then there have been a number of reports that suggest a genetic inheritance of this sort quite strongly.

In general, the findings have been that unipolar psychoses and bipolar psychoses appear to breed true with very little overlap. The percentages of affected family members vary. Angst found the percentage of affected family members in bipolar psychosis as 14.4% (parents) and 21.5% (sibs), and in unipolar psychosis 11.2% (parents) and 12.2% (sibs).

Twin studies suggest a concordance rate of around 70% in monozygotic and 19% in dizygotic twins of the same sex.

This strongly suggests a genetic influence in bipolar and unipolar psychoses which have been shown to breed true and which are relatively easy to identify. The mode of inheritance is not known, the majority view at present is that it is probably a polygenic type of inheritance.

There is no evidence of genetic factors operating in neurotic depression.

Chapter 2

Sex

In Western culture women are more frequently affected than men, with ratio of 2:1.

Social class

Hitherto it was held that affective disorders are more common in social classes I and II of the population, in contrast to schizophrenia, which is more common in social classes IV and V; it should be remembered that more subtle social factors may operate at least to some extent. In the 'upper' social classes depression may be more likely to be recognized by patient and doctor. That this can be the case in America, at any rate, was shown by Hollingshead & Redlich (1958) who demonstrated that diagnosis and treatment were materially affected by membership of a particular social class. Upper class people were found to be more likely to be diagnosed as neurotic and receive psychotherapy, while lower class people were more likely to be diagnosed as psychotic and receive E.C.T., and these biases appeared to be determined by social class. More recent population studies in the U.K. have indicated an increased incidence in working class females, particularly those with two or more children. An incidence as high as 15–20% of the population studied.

Current findings favour a significantly higher incidence of depressive states in lower socio-economic groups no matter how they are defined.

Constitution

1 *Body type.* The body type is more predominantly 'pyknic', i.e. small extremities and large visceral cavities (Mr Pickwick).
2 *Personality.* A personality type notable for swings of mood 'cyclothymic' personality is a common accompaniment of affective disorder.

Many patients who develop mania have a premorbid personality notable for unusual jollity and energy—the so-called hypomanic personality.

Stress

The relationship of depression to apparent external causes is often obscure and misleading—causes invoked by patient or relative may be no more than an expression of the illness itself. For example, a man presented with a history of depression after dismissal from his job. On closer questioning it became clear that his symptoms of depression had antedated his sacking and that he had lost his job because of his incompetence, itself a manifestation of depression.

Age

Age plays a part in the aetiology of depression, some age groups being particularly vulnerable. Old age with loneliness and the fear of death is the most obvious example. Middle age can be particularly threatening, particularly for the striving man who suddenly arrives at this age and realizes he has accomplished less than he hoped. If this coincides with the loss of his children by marriage etc., it is liable to be all the harder to bear and frank depression may develop. Adolescence is a time of turmoil and depression at this age, though rare, when it does occur is severe. The most severe depressions occur after age 60.

Physiological events precipitating depression

1 *Childbirth is the first and most obvious example*—An event of physiological and psychological significance. Lability of mood is normal in the puerperium, but acute severe depression does occur and needs prompt recognition and treatment.
2 The *menopause* is a time of hormonal and psychological change and is often accompanied by depression.
3 *Acute febrile illnesses*, such as influenza, can trigger off depression.
4 *Chronic illness*, particularly chronic painful illness is commonly accompanied by depression. Unfortunately this depression often passes unrecognized since such depression can be relieved and the illness made more easy to bear.
5 *Jaundice*.

Social factors

Social isolation and insecurity with loneliness and accompanying despair probably account for a large proportion of chronic depression.

Drugs

Many drugs can cause depression, including the sulphonamides, methyl dopa, reserpine, phenobarbitone and any of the contraceptive pills, particularly those with a high progesterone content. Steroids can cause depression—usually during withdrawal, and depressive states are common in withdrawal from amphetamines. Also, certain anti-Parkinsonian drugs, such as Benzhexol, may cause depression or even states of excitement and confusion.

Clinical manifestations

Mood change

Mood change is fundamental in every depressive illness. Here it is worth noting that one should not confuse the lay and medical usage of the term 'depression'. When we talk of depression we refer to a clinical entity and do not use it loosely to describe transitory feelings of sadness or dejection.

The depressed patient's mood colours his entire mental life; thus in severe depression he will form incorrect judgements—delusional ideas based on his altered mood—e.g. saying that he has been condemned to death for his numerous misdeeds.

Such severe depression is not common, what is much more common is a general depressive colouring to the patient's outlook. The world seems grey and dark to him, his future appears grim and he sees himself as a failure, unworthy of anyone's pity or affection. People who feel like this are likely to attempt suicide. Ideas of guilt and unworthiness are extremely common in depression.

Psychomotor activity

Alteration in psychomotor activity follows in the wake of mood change. The patient's movements and talk are slow and ponderous. This is called retardation. The patient is aware of this and often describes slowness in thought and difficulty in concentration. These latter can be elicited by simple tests of concentration, such as the serial subtraction of 7 from 100.

Poor concentration shows itself in the patient's work or studies and is confirmed by colleagues who tell him that he is not coping as well with his work as formerly. The housewife finds that work piles up in the home whilst she sits around in a hopeless state unable to concentrate but feeling sad and dejected. Frank weeping is not particularly common in depression. Far more common is the statement 'I've got past the stage of being able to cry. I can't cry any more. Perhaps I'd feel better if I could'.

Sleep disturbance

Insomnia is very common in depression and may be manifest as delayed sleep, broken sleep or early waking. Early waking is said to be the most common form of peristent sleep disorder. The patient wakes in the early hours and is unable to sleep, thereafter he remains awake for a few hours till he gets up unrefreshed. Often he has bad dreams.

Other bodily disturbances

By day the patient lacks energy, interest and appetite. Weight loss is common. Apathy and loss of interest may be the presenting symptoms of depression. Hypochondriacal concern is commonly found, particularly centring on the bowels which are often constipated.

Other psychological accompaniments

Anxiety is encountered in almost every depressive illness—there is no point in attempting clinical separation of anxiety from depression. Elderly depressed patients usually show agitation, that is to say restless semi-purposive overactivity with hand wringing and inability to sit or lie still. Agitation can sometimes be so severe as to resemble manic excitement, except that the affect is one of hopelessness and despair. Paranoid features, particularly in middle-aged and elderly patients, may dominate the clinical picture in depression.

Hysterical symptoms can either mask depression or complicate the picture. In the first instance failure to recognize the essential depressive nature of the illness can be very dangerous, particularly when the hysterical symptom is protecting the patient from a suicidal impulse.

Hypochondriasis is extremely common in depressive states—in its most severe form one finds hypochondriacal delusions in the severely depressed patient, more common perhaps is the finding of a pervasive hypochondriacal attitude in the concern about the bodily accompaniments of depression, such as constipation, etc. Very often this hypochondriasis is the presenting symptom of depression and may bring the patient initially to the attention of an investigating physician rather than a psychiatrist.

In summary, it can be said that current views on the symptomatology of major depressive illnesses in those that some would describe as endogenous, psychotic or primary are:

1   an autonomous cause;
2   a need for biological treatment; and
3   a presumed alteration in brain biochemistry.

There is now solid evidence to suggest that the primary and most important symptoms in these major depressive states are psychomotor retardation, agitation, feelings of self blame and decreased concentration in addition to mood change.

Differential diagnosis

Important physical disorders to be excluded are:

1   *Myxoedema.* Remembering that in myxoedema, depression and paranoid psychoses are commonly manifestations of the underlying disorder.
2   *Parkinsonism.* Depression is a common accompaniment of Parkinsonism.
3   *Myasthenia gravis.*
4   *Addison's disease.*

The important psychiatric conditions to be distinguished from depression are:

1   *Schizophrenia.* Though the presence of thought disorder and true delusions may make the diagnosis of schizophrenia on occasions comparatively simple, it has to be remembered that the prodroma of schizophrenia may be apparently entirely depressive, hence adolescent depression should be diagnosed very cautiously.
2   *Dementia.* Presence of signs of organic deterioration should make diagnosis of dementia possible, though atypical depressions may simulate dementia and depression may complicate dementia.

Complications of depression

1   Suicide and attempted suicide

All depressed patients should be carefully assessed for the possibility of suicide. Threats should never be ignored and must always be carefully evaluated. It is very important always to remember that there are a number of rather foolish statements about suicide which have been made which must be disregarded. First of these is 'if a patient talks about suicide they won't do it', nothing could be further from the truth. There are some generally agreed pointers which may indicate an impending suicidal attempt, and they include severe sleep disturbance with increased concern about it; history of previous suicidal attempt; a family history of suicide; suicidal talk and preoccupation; severe hypochondriasis; associated physical illness; social isolation, persistent feelings of guilt and self-depreciation.

In recent years the taking of tablets in the form of deliberate overdose has become so common in hospital practice that some have suggested that the term attempted suicide for these people should be discarded and that this should be referred to as self-poisoning. At all events, whatever the condition is called, it should always be remembered that from time to time people will take sleeping pills, etc. in doses in excess of therapeutic level in an attempt to blot out reality by deep sleep and also as a way of drawing attention to their personal or social problems. This is not to suggest that all suicidal attempts constitute a serious psychiatric emergency, but rather that everyone of these attempts should be evaluated by the physician with careful regard to the individual's personal and social situation.

2 Malnutrition

3 Worsening of co-existing physical disease

This may occur through neglect etc., e.g. pulmonary tuberculosis, diabetes mellitus.

4 Abuse of drugs or alcohol

This may happen in an attempt to 'fight off' depression.

Treatment

Of all psychiatric disorders depression is the most treatable. Nowadays the majority of depressives are treated as outpatients, but admission to hospital will always be necessary for severe depression, particularly where there is suicidal risk.

General measures

In the present era of physical treatments, the possibility of spontaneous remission is not awaited since most psychiatrists rightly feel that the patient's suffering should not be needlessly prolonged.

However, it should be remembered that good psychiatric nursing and sedation will always provide comfort and some degree of improvement to the depressed patient.

Physical treatment

1   *Electro-convulsive therapy (E.C.T.)* E.C.T. is widely regarded as a very useful antidepressant treatment in severe depressive states, but with the advent of the antidepressant drugs its usage has fallen off. Also, many psychiatrists are beginning seriously to question the value of E.C.T. (see Chapter 12).

2   *Anti-depressant drugs.* The antidepressant drugs include the tricyclic antidepressants and the monoamine oxidase inhibitors. Some of these medications are discussed more fully in Chapter 12. In general the tricyclic drugs are much more widely used than the monoamine oxidase inhibitors which have serious disadvantages from the point of view of side-effects and it appears that the latter type of drug has a much less definite place in the treatment of depression. It should be added that at the present time too, the place of the tricyclic antidepressants is being questioned by many since it is possible that they are being excessively used. Nevertheless, the antidepressant drugs remain the mainstay of the treatment of depression.

3   *Psychotherapy.* Usually supportive.

4   *Occupational therapy.*

5   *Social rehabilitation.*

6   *Cognitive therapy* (see Chapter 12).

Prognosis

Depression tends to recur. It may well be that prolonged medication with antidepressant drugs helps to avert recurrence, though it is too early to be definite about this. The average duration of hospitalization in depression is about 6 weeks.

MANIA

Mania is less common than depression and tends to be an acute and more circumscribed illness. Chronic depression is commonplace—chronic mania does not exist.

Hypomania is the term used to describe mild or moderate degrees of mania.

Aetiology

1 See depression.
2 *Pre-morbid personality.* Commonly the manic patient is found to have either a cyclothymic personality or else to have always been more energetic and cheerful than his fellows (hypomanic personality).

Clinical manifestations

Mood

The mood is one of cheerfulness—or hilarity. Manic patients are described as showing infectious jollity—soon everyone in the room is laughing with them. This is often true, but the jollity is more often than not well laced with irritability and flashes of anger, particularly if someone disagrees with the patient. The manic patient denies all symptoms and says he has never felt better in his life. He is optimistic and has elaborate plans for the future, not only his future but for anyone else who cares to take advantage of the plans he is making. The plans at first may be sensible, if a little overenthusiastically stated, but sooner or later they become grandiose as the patient's critical sense fades. The patient's insight about his lack of judgement is practically nil in mania. Sudden mood changes with transient bouts of tearful sadness are also encountered.

Activity

The overactivity in mania follows naturally from the feeling of general well-being that the patient experiences. His energy is boundless. He gets up before everyone else in the house and goes to bed long after exhausted members of the family have retired. At work he goes from one project to another, completing nothing. He overspends, buys all sorts of things, dresses extravagantly and invites large numbers of unexpected friends home. As activity increases, so the patient's attention decreases so that he is able to concentrate less on anything.

Talk

Talk reflects the cheery mood and increased activity. The stream of talk gradually increases till it becomes torrential. It flits from topic to topic (flight of ideas), and associations are casual, often triggered by rhymes or puns. Jokes are frequent.

Delusions

True delusions are not found but the manic patient does form delusional ideas based on his overoptimistic views of life in general. It is also not uncommon to find the irritable manic showing a paranoid attitude, particularly when any objections are made to his plans.

Bodily disturbance

1 Sleep is lost through excessive energy.
2 Appetite is often voracious without any weight gain.
3 Libido is heightened.
4 Abuse of alcohol is common.

Mode of onset

Onset is usually acute and the duration of a manic illness is on the average about 6–8 weeks.

Hypomania often passes unrecognized at first, it is merely remarked by relatives that the patient had seemed full of zest and cheeriness for a few weeks and then things seemed to get out of hand.

Some manic illnesses terminate abruptly, others swing into depression.

Diagnosis

1 *Schizophrenic and schizo-affective psychoses.* The presence of true thought disorder and delusions should make simple the diagnosis of

these from mania. In practice it is often difficult to be precise about states of excitement. Time usually clarifies the picture.

2 *Drug-induced excitement,* e.g. amphetamine and its derivatives.

Treatment

1 *Admission to hospital.*

2 *Attention to feeding, etc.* The manic patient may be so overactive that he stops eating for a few days before admission. This means that he arrives in hospital exhausted and dehydrated. As a consequence his mental state may be the more disturbed through vitamin depletion.

3 *Medication.* (a) Sedatives. Immediate sedation to calm a wildly excited patient can be used, but this has generally been replaced by the use of neuroleptics.

(b) Neuroleptics. Neuroleptic drugs are extremely useful in calming manic excitement and those most commonly used include: (i) Chlor-promazine—up to 1 g per 24 hours in divided doses; (ii) Thioridazine (Melleril); (iii) Haloperidol—the starting dose of haloperidol given to an excited patient may be 5 mg intramuscularly and, thereafter, the dose repeated every hour until the patient has calmed down. After this the patient can usually be managed on much smaller doses by mouth.

4 *E.C.T.* E.C.T. has a definite place in the treatment of mania. It is usually given with neuroleptics.

5 *Lithium.* Lithium was first recognized as a psychotropic drug as long ago as 1897, had a bad reputation for toxicity until 1949 when interest in its use was revived. Present uses are: (a) treatment of acute manic states; (b) treatment of recurrent manic states; (c) treatment of chronic depressive states.

In the case of acute mania it appears to have a definite place, though its value in recurrent mania, i.e. as a prophylactic drug, is less certain. Its place in the treatment of chronic depression is very uncertain. The drug is given as lithium carbonate, usually at a dose of 300–600 mg t.d.s., levelling off to a lower maintenance dose. Its toxic effects necessitate frequent monitoring of the serum lithium level which should not rise above 1.6–1.9 mEql. Toxic effects include: (a) gastro-intestinal effects—anorexia, nausea, vomiting and diarrhoea; (b) neuromuscular effects—weakness, tremor, ataxia and choreoathetosis; (c) C.N.S. effects—incontinence, dysarthria, blurred vision, dizziness, fits, retardation, somnolence and confusion, stupor, coma; (d) cardiovascular effects—pulse irregularities, E.C.G. changes, circulatory collapse.

Other effects: polyuria, polydipsia, dehydration.

Because of its toxicity, lithium should not be given to anyone with any degree of renal impairment. And in general it is a drug that should only be used in the setting of inpatient and outpatient hospital care.

Conclusion

In general, of the affective disorders it can be said that depression is a common disorder which is amenable to treatment by a wide variety of methods and is one which can cause a great deal of hardship, and for this reason should not pass unrecognized. In the treatment of depression a good rule to abide by is that if the patient is not showing improvement with a particular line of treatment, this line of treatment should not be pushed to the level of absurdity before trying something else.

REFERENCES

Brown G. W., Brohclain M. N. & Harris T. (1975) Social Class and Psychiatric Disturbance Among Women in an Urban Population. *Sociol.*, **9**, 35.

Hollingshead A. B. & Redlich F.C. (1958) *Social Class and Mental Illness: a Community Study.* John Wiley & Son, New York.

Kendell R. E. (1976) The classification of depressions: A review of contemporary confusion. *Br. J. Psychiat.*, **139**, 15.

Kiloh L. & Garside R. F. (1963) Independence of neurotic depression and endogenous depression. *Br. J. Psychiat.*, **109**, 451.

Kraepelin E. (1921) *Manic Depressive Insanity and Paranoia.* Churchill-Livingstone, Edinburgh.

Lewis A. J. (1934) Melancholia. A clinical survey of depressive states. *J. Ment. Sci.*, **80**, 277.

Medical Research Council (1965). Clinical trial of the treatment of depressive illness. *Br. Med. J.*, **i**, 881.

Nelson J. C. & Charney D. S. (1981) The symptoms of major depressive illness. *Am. J. Psychiat.*, **138**, 1.

Nelson J. C. & Charney D. S. (1980) Primary affective disorder criteria and the endogenous-reactive distinction. *Arch. Gen. Psychiatry*, **37**, 787.

Storey P. B. (1968) Pathogenetic and other aspects of depression. *Br. J. Hosp. Med.*, **4**, 1157.

Watts C. A. H. (1966) *Depressive Disorders in the Community.* John Wright, Bristol.

Winokur G. & Pitts F. N. (1964) Affective disorders: 1. Is reactive depression an entity? *J. Nerv. Ment. Dis.*, **138**, 541.

CHAPTER 3
SCHIZOPHRENIA

Definition

Schizophrenia is a syndrome in which are found specific psychological manifestations recognizable clinically, occurring before age 45 and commonly leading to disintegration of the personality. The schizophrenic has peculiar ways of thinking and behaving and perceives his environment in an abnormal way. He has an inner life dominated by fantastic ideas, his emotional display is incongruous and he is cut off from his fellows so that he appears to have withdrawn from the world. The syndrome was originally described by Kraepelin (1896) who delineated its essentials under the name 'Dementia Praecox'. This was a fundamental step in the history of descriptive psychiatry since up till that time what we now recognize as schizophrenia was buried in a multitude of apparently dissimilar syndromes. The name 'Schizophrenia' was applied by Bleuler who viewed the syndrome as being based on a process of psychological disintegration manifesting itself ultimately as a fragmentation of the personality.

Aetiology

Incidence

The incidence of schizophrenia is found to be 0.85% of the general population. This figure is remarkably constant whatever populations are surveyed.

Heredity

The precise role of heredity in schizophrenia is uncertain and the means of inheritance is unknown. It is possible to calculate the expectancy of schizophrenia in the family of the schizophrenic, where the incidence in the proband's parents may be between 5–10% and in full sibs 5–15%.

Twin studies used to be quoted as showing a concordance rate of up to 80% in monozygotic twins but the figure is now said to be 60%, though some put the figure as low as 30%. Schizophrenia breeds true in families; on the other hand 60% of schizophrenics have no family history. Two recent studies support a genetic factor in schizophrenia. They both concern adopted children. Heston and Denney (1968) traced forty-seven adopted children of schizophrenic mothers compared to fifty controls children of non-psychotic mothers and found the first group were significantly more disturbed on six indices of major psychosocial disorders including five who were schizophrenic. Rosenthal *et al.* (1971) studied 5500 adopted children and compared the incidence of schizophrenia in children of psychotic as compared to non-psychotic parents and found three schizophrenics in the index children, none in the controls and 31.6% 'schizophrenia spectrum disorder' in the index group as opposed to 17.8% in the controls.

Personality

Many writers have stressed the importance of the pre-morbid personality structure of the schizophrenic. As ever one is confronted with the difficulty of assessing personality but even so a 'schizoid personality' has been described. This is a personality type which appears to contain the seeds of schizophrenia. Schizoid individuals display behavioural traits such as seclusiveness, abnormal shyness, hypochondriasis, emotional coolness and indifference, fanaticism and eccentricity. However there is some difference found by various workers in the incidence of these abnormal personalities before the onset of schizophrenia. Bleuler found a 34% incidence of schizoid personality in a series of schizophrenics. Other workers have found a higher incidence but it has to be admitted that up to 50% of schizophrenics show no evidence of previous personality disorder. Nevertheless the finding of personality disorder in an individual suspected of the slow development of schizophrenia may be a useful pointer toward the diagnosis. Further evidence of the role played by personality abnormality in the aetiology of schizophrenia is demonstrated by the increased incidence of deviant individuals in the families of schizophrenics.

Body-build

The incidence of the asthenic body structure has been commented on by many workers. This type of body-build is of poor prognostic significance—tending to be associated with chronicity.

Childhood experience

Important theories of family processes in the aetiology of schizophrenia are the 'double bind theory' of Bateson *et al.* (1956) and that of Lidz *et al.* (1966).

Bateson *et al.* postulated a family situation in which the young child is commands containing implied negatives, i.e. ordering the child to disobey the orders given.

In this situation the victim can expect punishment whatever he does: moreover he may expect punishment if he makes no choice and takes no action. The theory extrapolates from this to a situation where the child learns to avoid punishment by making meaningless remarks and comes to behave as if he can no longer understand others, i.e. becomes schizophrenic.

Lidz and co-workers postulate the importance of a family situation in which the family as a whole displays pathological patterns of thought, behaviour and view of the world in general.

Laing and Esterson (1964) have pointed out that a family may pressurize a member into a psychotic position by ensnaring him in a net of ambiguity, which leaves him no alternative but to act in a way that may seem odd or 'psychotic' but is actually his only way of self-preservation in a malign family situation.

It is difficult to evaluate these theories of schizophrenic aetiology but it should not be thought that their explanatory and speculative nature makes them in any way mutually exclusive as compared with biological theories. Far from it, schizophrenia is a heterogeneous collection of syndromes and no unitary theory of causality is acceptable on the evidence presently available.

Biochemistry

There is a growing body of evidence to suggest that the disturbance of schizophrenia may be biochemically transmitted. It has to be conceded that to date no specific biochemical defect has been identified as having an exclusive association with schizophrenia. Production of the so-called 'model psychoses' in volunteers following the administration of lysergic acid diethylamide and mescaline was probably the first step in the investigation of the biochemistry of schizophrenia. However, perhaps the foremost indication of a biochemical disturbance and a neuro-pathological disturbance in the aetiology of schizophrenia was provided first of all by the recognition of psychoses triggered off by taking amphetamines and secondly by the investigation of psychoses associated with temporal lobe epilepsy. In both these conditions, psychoses are produced which are clinically indistinguishable from schizophrenia. It was the further investigation of the amphetamine-induced psychoses that has led to the *dopamine hypothesis*. In this, it is postulated the symptoms of schizophrenia are related to a functional excess of struc-turally normal dopamine. Amphetamines induce dopamine overactivity while at the same time it is found that antipsychotic drugs reduce it presumably by blocking dopamine receptors. Biochemical hypotheses of schizophrenia have included the transmethylation hypothesis in which it is proposed that schizophrenic symptoms are caused by the accumulation of an abnormal biogenic amine. Other lines of enquiry relate to the possibility that schizophrenia is in fact an encephalitis produced by a slow virus and in addition to this considerable interest has been raised by finding ventricular dilatation in chronic schizophrenics indicating a degree of cerebral atrophy which could well be related to a slow virus disorder.

Physical illness

Physical happenings such as illnesses, operations or accidents can commonly precipitate an acute schizophrenic psychosis or bring about remission in an established one.

Life changes

Recent research suggests that schizophrenic onset and relapse are significantly preceded by life changes such as moving house, loss of a job, bereavement etc. The implication of this may be that the schizo-phrenic has a low tolerance for change or overstimulation.

Psychological factors

The role of psychological factors in the aetiology of schizophrenia is far from clear. Common clinical experience teaches us that the schizo-phrenic may have the illness triggered off by any variety of psychological stress.

A comprehensive theory of the aetiology of schizophrenia would postulate that the schizophrenic process is mediated biochemically, i.e. follows a biochemical final common path, that the illness occurs in a genetically predisposed individual, and that this disturbance may be triggered off by a variety of physical or psychological stresses or both. It would certainly seem at the present time that this theory of multiple aetiology would be the most profitable one to follow in research.

Schizophrenia therefore, appears to be a complex disturbance occurring at many levels in which hereditary, psychological, neurophysiological, sociological and biochemical factors may all play relevant parts.

Clinical manifestations

These are best considered under the following headings: thought disorder; delusions; emotional disturbance; perceptual disturbance; and behavioural disturbance.

The reason for commencing with thought disorder lies in the fact that Bleuler in his original description of schizophrenia stressed the central position of the disturbance of thinking found in schizophrenia.

Schizophrenic thought disorder

This is a characteristic disturbance of the thought process peculiar to the schizophrenic syndrome. The schizophrenic's powers of thinking are impaired, i.e. his powers of *conceptual thinking are altered,* so that he may interchange cause and effect and draw entirely illogical conclusions from false premises. This will manifest itself by the finding that his talk is difficult to follow. When one examines an example of this talk one finds that the patient has said much but got little across. Closer examination reveals he has uttered a stream of nonsense. Subjectively the patient may be aware of impaired thinking ability and may tell the examiner that he finds it hard to think clearly or that his thoughts are vague, or that he cannot concentrate, or that somehow his thoughts wander. It may be necessary to use leading questions to elicit this information from a patient. As thought disorder is manifest in language, it has been suggested that the schizophrenic is forced to construct for himself a private language to explain his illogical ideas to himself and others.

Attention is often drawn to the phenomenon of *thought blocking.* Here the patient's stream of thought is interrupted, and a new line of thinking begins. It is shown by gaps in the patient's talk and found too in states of exhaustion and depressive retardation. Thought blocking is therefore *not peculiar* to *schizophrenia*. All the foregoing comments on schizo-phrenic thought disorder presuppose that the individual is of adequate intelligence. The diagnosis of schizophrenic thought disorder in the presence of subnormal intelligence would be extremely difficult.

The schizophrenic may experience interruption of thinking and tell the examiner that his *thoughts are being withdrawn* (thought withdrawal) from his head, or that thoughts are being inserted into his head. This sort of complaint is absolutely diagnostic of schizophrenia and occurs in no other condition. In addition, he may experience transmission of his own thoughts to others. The term 'schizophrenic thought disorder' refers to the *specific disturbance of conceptual thinking* mentioned at the beginning of this section.

Delusions

A delusion is defined as an incorrect belief which is inappropriate to the individual's socio-cultural background, and which is held in the fact of logical argument. True delusions are fundamental errors in judgement and are as inexplicable as they are incomprehensible. They appear suddenly and are held with particular conviction. A distinction is drawn between these true or primary delusions and delusional ideas, since primary delusions are completely incomprehensible whereas delusional ideas are false but nevertheless explicable in the light of the patient's altered emotional state. For instance, in severe depression an individual can develop delusional ideas which can be explained on the grounds of his being sad and therefore believing that his life is finished, his future is hopeless etc. The delusion proper is unshakeable and incorrect and held without insight. The content of a patient's delusion reflects his past experience and is coloured by his culture pattern. Thus 100 years ago religious content in delusions was much more common than it is at the moment. Nowadays it is common for deluded patients to believe that they are being persecuted by political organizations such as the Fascists, Communists etc., or that they are being influenced by atomic explos-ions, radioactivity, radar, television etc. A deluded patient may also experience *ideas of reference*. This is an experience in which the patient finds that mundane happenings of even the most trifling sort have special meaning and significance for him or are directed particularly towards him. Thus a patient has found references to herself in the personal column of *The Times*, or another patient turned on a TV programme and found that all the characters were making remarks about him. *Passivity feelings* are commonly found in schizophrenia. In this the individual feels that his body or mind are under the influence of or being controlled by other people. Though paranoid delusions are not always present in a schizophrenic illness, a paranoid colouring is common.

Emotional disturbance

Affective incongruity is typically found in severe schizophrenic illnesses. In this the patient's emotional display is inappropriate to his condition. In its most crude form one finds a patient laughing callously when being given some tragic news, or talking of some serious happening. In the majority of instances we find that the emotional incongruity of schizophrenia is not so marked as the lack of emotional rapport which one can make with a schizophrenic. Many people have spoken of the pane of glass which separates one from the schizophrenic patient. It is difficult to identify with or empathize with a schizophrenic. His emotional display is limited: he is cool detached, rather 'couldn't care less'. He is unmoved by the various things going on around him and concerned only with his own private world. Other variations of emotion are found in schizophrenia too. It is not uncommon for a schizophrenic illness to be ushered in by a state of depression or anxiety or even mild hypomanic excitement. In fact it is fair to say that any young patient, i.e. adolescent patient, who presents with severe anxiety, inexplicable depression or acute hypomanic excitement must be suspected of a developing schizophrenia until it has been proven otherwise.

Perceptual disturbance

The commonest perceptual disturbance of schizophrenia is the hallucination which is most commonly auditory. It is important always to enquire closely into the content and nature of the hallucinations. Patients may hear voices commenting on their actions, speaking their own thoughts aloud, uttering obscene words or phrases or telling them what to do. The voices may be familiar or unfamiliar, single or multiple. The majority of schizophrenic patients develop hallucinations at one stage or another during the illness.

Behavioural disturbance

In the development of schizophrenia one looks for alteration of the total behaviour of the individual rather than isolated phenomena. Often the relatives will describe how the individual has become more and more seclusive over a period of months, has appeared odd and made use of unfamiliar gestures, has shunned friends and familiar activities. States of ecstasy, wild excitement and impulsive behaviour also occur in schizophrenia but probably the most common finding is a general falling off in activity. The scholar becomes less studious and the professional man less interested and able to perform his work. Periods of apparent inactivity may be interspersed with occasional bouts of rather purposeless enthusiasm for some hobby or other. Thus a schizophrenic was said to be spending much time on 'research'. When investigated this turned out to be a method of preserving butterflies' wings in some plastic substance which was somehow allied to a thesis on biochemistry. Outbursts of violence or senseless criminal acts are fortunately rare but can occur. Altered moral standards may be seen in developing schizophrenia, thus a younger girl previously puritanical may become promiscuous, and it may be this concern about her sexual morals which brings her parents to consult the doctor, and the diagnosis of schizophrenia made. Any history of personality change in a young person must always raise the suspicion of schizophrenia.

Clinical types

Nowadays less importance is attached to the naming of clinical types. The making of the diagnosis, indeed establishing the concept of schizophrenia, is often hard enough!

The clinical types which are described include:

1 *Simple schizophrenia.* Simple schizophrenia is characterized by a general lowering of all mental activity. The simple schizophrenic presents with poverty of activity, volition, affect and thought. This variety of schizophrenia is most commonly confused with mental subnormality. Indeed the two clinical pictures may be indistinguishable. The onset is usually slow and insidious and the prognosis in general very bad.

2 *Hebephrenia.* As its name implies this is seen in the younger age groups and typically the clinical picture is one of rather fatuous euphoria

and hallucinosis. Here the onset tends to be insidious and the prognosis bad. Thought disorder is usually marked.

3 *Paranoid schizophrenia.* Characterized by the development of systems of paranoid delusions. The onset is slow and insidious. Paranoid schizophrenia is often associated with considerable preservation of the personality, so that the paranoid schizophrenic may be able to remain for a considerable time in the community and conceal his paranoid delusions. It is found in older age groups (30 and over).

The term *catatonic* has been abandoned. Formerly used to describe a clinical type of schizophrenia it is now recognized that the term, used to encompass states of stupor or excitement was not specific to schizophrenia but was a manifestation of organic brain disease, affective disorder or schizophrenia.

General comments on diagnosis

A central problem in the diagnosis of schizophrenia has been the poor level of agreement amongst psychiatrists about definition of the term. Essentially schizophrenia comprises:

1   certain psychotic features such as delusions, thought disorder, hallucinations and emotional blunting;
2   a deterioration in function;
3   onset before age 45;
4   a duration measured in months rather than days.

The lack of agreement on definition has led to the development of ten different operational definitions, one of which, that of Feighner is as follows.

Feighner's definition of schizophrenia:
A–C required.
A   (1) A chronic illness with at least 6 months of symptoms without return to the pre-morbid level of adjustment; and
(2) absence of a period of depressive or manic symptoms sufficient to qualify for affective disorder or probable affective disorder.
B   At least one of:
(1) delusions or hallucinations without significant perplexity or disorientation; or
(2) verbal production that makes communication difficult because of lack of logical or understandable organization.

C   At least three of:
    (1) single state;
    (2) poor pre-morbid social adjustment or work history;
    (3) family history of schizophrenia;
    (4) absence of alcoholism or drug abuse within 1 year of onset of the
    psychosis; or
    (5) onset of illness prior to age 40.
    If only two present, 'probable' schizophrenia.

On the other hand, Schneider (1959) stressed the importance of 'first
rank symptoms', *viz.* audible thoughts, voices heard arguing, voices
commenting on one's actions, the experience of influences playing on
the body (somatic passivity experiences), thought withdrawal and other
interferences with thought; diffusion of thought, delusional perception
and all feelings, impulses (drives) and volitional acts that are experienced by the patient as the work or influence of others.
    Definition and diagnosis then, are far from satisfactory but they are
improving. This author tends to the use of Schneider's criteria and
observing the evolution of the disorder. The development of the disorder is often the best pointer to the diagnosis.

Differential diagnosis

1   *Affective disorder.*
2   *Drug-induced psychosis.* e.g. Amphetamines, LSD or other hallucinogenic drugs.
3   *Organic psychosis.* Here the presence of clouded consciousness will
be the critical diagnostic point.
4   *Personality disorder.*
5   *Hysteria.*
6   *Paranoid states.* Not everyone who becomes paranoid is schizophrenic!
7   *Psychosis associated with epilepsy.*

Treatment

No psychiatric topic is more beset with pitfalls than the treatment of
schizophrenia. Since this is a poorly comprehended condition it is
therefore difficult to treat adequately and impossible to treat specifically.
This leads on the one hand to therapeutic nihilism and neglect of the

patient and on the other to over treatment based on tenuous theory making the syndrome a perpetual testing ground. It is difficult to know which is the more dangerous of the two alternatives.

The treatment of the schizophrenic patient should consist of *a total approach to the patient*, aiming at strengthening his ties with reality and rehabilitating him. In the acute state of the illness the patient may need to be in hospital and may have to be protected from himself since suicide commonly occurs in schizophrenia—he may need to be calmed by sedatives and tranquillizers, and his general state of health may need investigation, for co-existing physical diseases which, if found are appropriately treated.

At the present time the phenothiazine drugs, particularly *chlorpromazine* and *trifluoperazine*, are found particularly useful to influence the mental state of the schizophrenic. These drugs not only calm but also alter perception and modify thinking. Chlorpromazine is given orally (50–200 mg t.d.s.) or by injection. *Trifluoperazine* is given orally (5–15 mg t.d.s.). Intramuscular injection of fluphenazine deanoate (Modecate) 25 mg once monthly is now established as an effective medication which many now regard as the treatment of choice. Dystonic and other extrapyramidal reactions are common but usually respond well to antiparkinsonian drugs.

The use of E.C.T. in schizophrenia is controversial. Certainly it is of value in a schizophrenic illness of acute onset, and where affective features are present.

Psychotherapy plays a part in the treatment of schizophrenia. It is of a supportive and re-integrative rather than analytic type. A psychotic patient cannot tolerate interpretations of his behaviour, and indeed such therapy can often be dangerously disruptive.

It is important to find useful and variable occupation for the patient. This may start with traditional occupational therapy. On the other hand there is much evidence to suggest that occupation of a constructive sort may be particularly valuable. The current interest in the reclamation of the chronic schizophrenic has shown the value of 'industrial therapy'. In industrial therapy units, chronic schizophrenics perform meaningful tasks producing various objects, e.g. light industrial assembly work etc., emphasis being placed on making the situation as near to a normal work situation as possible. This encourages the patient to adopt a normal working role, and prepares him for a return to the community and the consequent return to gainful occupation.

Community care

No schizophrenic patient can be adequately treated in a social vacuum. For this reason it is important for the doctor concerned to know as much as possible about the patient's family and home conditions. The patient who comes from a family in which there are close ties and supportive interest is liable to make better progress than the patient who is socially isolated.

Community care should therefore be more comprehensive than hospital care and is based on outpatient clinics and day hospitals. The object of community care is to avoid hospital admission wherever possible in order to avert the institutionalized apathy that the schizophrenic can so readily develop.

The Mental Health Act has invested the local authority with the responsibility of organizing such services and in certain areas they are highly developed.

However there is always the danger that the patient may be over-looked if communication is poor and the general practitioner, the hospital doctors and the local authority each assume that the other two are looking after him. Well-organized community care involves highly developed social work by psychiatric social workers, mental welfare officers and others in collaboration with the hospital psychiatrists, general practitioners and community physicians. Ideally the whole operation should be part of a comprehensive, community-oriented mental health service.

There is much more to the follow up of patients discharged from hospital than mere attendance at an outpatient clinic now and again to receive further medication. The family of the schizophrenic patient require rather more than simple reassurance. The presence of a psychotic member in the family can be enormously disrupting and may evoke every sort of emotional response.

To ignore this and discharge a patient to an unprepared family is to invite early re-admission. It is worth noting too that patients *can* be neglected at home.

Treatment of the schizophrenic patient is often difficult and un-rewarding but chronicity can be avoided if emphasis is placed on strengthening the patient's ties with reality, i.e. with the community at large and facilitating his return to that community as soon as is reasonably possible and avoiding conditions of social neglect. There is much evidence to suggest that many of the features previously held to be typical of chronic schizophrenia are in fact features of social neglect.

Prognosis

Making an accurate prognosis of schizophrenia is difficult but there are a few useful pointers. The following features may be regarded as good prognostic signs.

1 Acute onset.
2 The presence of psychological or physical precipitants, e.g. childbirth, operations, etc.
3 Normal pre-morbid personality.
4 Stable social background, i.e. close social ties etc.
5 The presence of affective features.
6 Average or above average intelligence.

The following are poor prognostic features.

1 Insidious onset.
2 Persistent thought disorder.
3 Asthenic bodily habitus.
4 Presence of flattening of affect.
5 Subnormal intelligence.

REFERENCES

Bateson G., Jackson D. D., Haley J. & Weakland J. H. (1956) Toward a theory of schizophrenia. *Behav. Sci.* 1, 251–264.

Bowlby J. (1951) Maternal care and mental health. *W.H.O. Monogr. Ser. No. 2.*

Brockington I. F., Kendell R. E. & Leff J. P. (1978) Definitions of schizophrenia: concordance and predictions of outcome. *Phsychol. Med.,* 8, 387.

Brown G. W. & Birley J. L. T. (1968) Crises and life changes in the onset of schizophrenia. *J. Health Soc. Behav.,* 9, 203.

Feighner J. P., Robins E., Guze S. B., Woodruffe R. A., Winokur G. & Munoz R. (1972) Diagnostic criteria for use in psychiatric research. *Arch. Gen. Psychiatry,* 26, 57.

Fish F. J. (1959) What is Schizophrenia? *Med. Progr. (N.Y.),* 242, 97.

Fredrickson P. & Richelson E. (1979) Mayo Seminars in psychiatry: Dopamine and schizophrenia—a review. *J. Clin. Psychiatry,* 40, 399.

Kalmann F. J. (1946) The genetic theory of schizophrenia. *Am. J. Psychiatry,* 103, 309.

Kendell R. E. (1972) Schizophrenia: The remedy for diagnostic confusion. *Br. J. Hosp. Med.,* 8, 383.

Heston L. L. & Denney D. (1968) Interactions between early life experience and biological factors in schizophrenics. In *The Transmission of Schizophrenia.* (Eds D. Rosenthal & S. Kety) Pergamon Press, Oxford.

Kind H. (1966) The psychogenesis of schizophrenia—a review of the literature. *Br. J. Psychiatry,* 112, 333.

Laing R. D. & Esterson A. (1964) *Sanity, Madness and the Family.* Tavistock, London.
Langfeldt G. (1956) The prognosis of schizophrenia. *Acta Psychiat. Kbb,* Suppl. 110.
Lidz T., Flack S. & Cornelison (1966) *Schizophrenia in the Family.* International University Press Inc, New York.
Mishler E. G. & Scotch N. A. (1965) Sociocultural factors in the epidemiology of schizophrenia. *Int. J. Psychiat.,* 1, 258.
Rosenthal D., Wender P., Kety S., Wemer J., Schursinger F. (1971) The adopted-away offspring of schizophrenics. *Am. J. Psychiatry,* 128, 307.
Schneider K. (1959) *Clinical Psychopathology* (translated by M. W. Hamilton), 133–34. Grune and Stratton, London and New York.
Snyder S. H., Bannerjee S. P., Yamamura H. I. & Greenberg D. (1974) Drugs, neurotransmitters and schizophrenia. *Science,* 184, 1234.
Wing J. K. (1961) A simple and reliable subclassification of chronic schizophrenia. *J. ment. Sci.,* 107, 862.

CHAPTER 4
ORGANIC SYNDROMES
DEMENTIA, DELIRIUM AND ALLIED
STATES

Introduction

Disturbances of cerebral function consequent on gross physical or subtle neuro-chemical damage lead to recognizable disorders which are called 'organic syndromes'. In organic syndromes the predominant impairment is of *cognitive function.* Affective symptoms, anxiety etc. are purely secondary.

1 *Delirium and allied conditions* being characterized by

overactivity
clouded consciousness } acute delirium
hallucinosis

and

perplexity
clouded consiousness } subacute delirium ('confusional state')
incoherent thought

2 *Dementia.* (a) Primary where the cause is unknown and not secondary to some other metabolic or structural disturbance. Good examples of primary dementias are Huntington's chorea and Alzheimer's dementia.

(b) Secondary where the cause of dementia is known, e.g. atherosclerosis, producing multi infarct dementia, tumour, head injury.

DELIRIUM AND SUBACUTE DELIRIUM

Clinical manifestations

The most striking finding in states of delirium is the *impairment of consciousness.* In acute delirium this is severe—in its mildest form it is found in the feelings of 'muzziness in the head' that people experience in influenza, etc.

With impaired consciousness the individual's *awareness* of himself and of his surroundings is impaired. Also the level of wakefulness may be affected. The delirious child is often alarmingly bright-eyed and chatty. Wakefulness, on the other hand, may be reduced, producing a drowsy appearance. With impaired awareness and recognition of the surroundings is found *poor attention* and *concentration* so that a patient, when asked, cannot perform simple tasks such as washing or tying his pyjama cord without getting lost halfway through. He *cannot register* the information coming in from his environment so naturally fails in tests of memory of a simple sort.

Disorientation for time and place is invariably present and severe. *Perception* is altered, either subtly or grossly. Subtle perceptual alteration is usually first noticed by the patient saying that everything round seems clearer and sharper. Later in delirium, *gross perceptual errors* occur (illusions). When this happens the patient mistakes patterns on the wallpaper for insects and animals, shadows become menacing people and bedside consultations are heard as sinister plots. Finally the patient experiences *hallucinosis*. Visual hallucinations are common in delirium. They can take many forms. Perhaps the most common are small objects moving quickly across the visual field, e.g. in alcoholic delirium tremens patients often see small animals crawling all over the room. Hallucinations of this sort are described vividly by the patient and frequently appear clearly in his field of vision. Even their bizarre appearance is greeted without surprise, e.g. a patient recovering from chronic barbiturate intoxication saw a 6-inch-tall manikin running around the room and hiding under the floorboards. She identified it as her husband but could not understand why no one would let her prise up the floorboards to let him out. When prevented she became homicidally violent.

Motor disturbance in delirium varies from overactivity in acute delirium to mild irritability seen in subacute delirium. The severe overactivity can be prolonged and exhausting and represents a considerable physical hazard to the patient. The patient is restless, particularly at night, will not stay in bed, and is found wandering about the ward peering out of windows, searching and muttering to himself. He insists on leaving the ward; he must go to work; he makes a collection of his belongings, arranges and rearranges them, but such is his incoherent thinking that it all gets in a muddle and he starts all over again.

Emotional symptoms are common. States of panic and terror are usually abrupt in onset, the patient acting under the influence of his misperception of his environment. *Milder emotional symptoms* are often missed; this is unfortunate because if recognized they are useful signposts. The mildly delirious patient feels *vaguely apprehensive and uncomfortable,* and cannot say why. This may be noticed by the nurses who are surprised to find Mr X unusually uncooperative, having refused his supper.

Delusional ideas in delirium are loose and unformulated and come from the chaotic perceptions that the patient experiences. They never have the clarity and conviction of true schizophrenic delusions.

Physical examination of the delirious patient may reveal common causes such as:
1   alcohol;
2   pneumonia; or
3   barbiturate intoxication (chronic),
but the delirious state itself induces secondary physical changes as the patient refuses food and fluids so that he may show signs of:
1   dehydration;
2   vitamin depletion;
and further psychological disturbance, so that a vicious circle is set up.

Diagnosis

The diagnosis of delirium is not difficult to make providing the examiner concentrates on establishing the state of consciousness and orientation for time and place. Impairment of consciousness and orientation do not occur in schizophrenia nor in mania.

Acute delirium is usually transient, subacute delirious states may last for weeks.

DEMENTIA

Clinical manifestations

In dementia there is *progressive and irreversible intellectual deterioration* consequent on brain damage. The damaged brain cannot absorb and store new information and this is manifest by *impairment of recent memory* which is usually the most striking finding. Patients may complain of this memory defect or it may be noticed by others and not mentioned by the patient. Often patients attempt to overcome this memory defect by keeping a notebook reminding them to do things; this is usually successful for a while but sooner or later the problem overwhelms him and he presents anxious and bewildered, fogged by a day's routine which he cannot recall. *Behaviour* shows a deterioration, *interest, activity* and *energy* fall off, the professional man copes less easily with his work, the housewife can not keep up with her chores, the gas is turned on but not lit. Unusual behaviours, e.g. masturbation, self-exposure, shoplifting, can appear as a release phenomenon and with its attendant legal consequences bring about the recognition of the underlying process. *The appearance* deteriorates, clothes become unkempt and stained with food. The decline is overall, leading ultimately to helpless incontinence. *Concentration* is impaired. This can be elicited easily by simple tests such as the serial subtraction of 7 from 100. The patient is often aware of his poor ability and becomes very upset, angry, tearful and agitated when he is confronted with a task which proves too much for him. This is called the *catastrophic reaction.*

The fundamental impairment of brain function in organic brain disease is well demonstrated when this occurs. Organic brain disease produces rigidity of thinking, impairment of grasp and consequent difficulty in problem solving. Psychological tests of brain damage are designed to search for this sort of dysfunction and also to demonstrate difficulty in shifting from abstract to concrete and vice versa.

Emotional changes in dementia

There are no specific emotional disturbances. They tend to reflect in an exaggerated form the individual's previous patterns of emotional display. Lability of mood is common as control weakens and in advanced dementia one finds states of 'emotional incontinence'. Depression is common and usually ascribed to the patient's awareness of his plight. *Hysterical symptoms* may appear early in a dementing process. It is suggested that they are caused by the lower order of central nervous control and integration brought about by brain damage.

Diagnosis

The diagnosis of dementia is not difficult when the clinical picture is typical. However, there are difficulties particularly when confronted with middle-aged patients in whom dementia may be suspected purely on the grounds of a history, say, of falling off of interest and energy for many months with some associated mood change. In such a case chronic depression may account for the whole illness, but this may not be so, and one may be left with a patient whom one has to keep under observation.

Aetiology of dementia and delirium

Having found signs of an organic mental state, one is next concerned with finding the underlying cause. The commonest factors causing organic mental syndromes include:

Cerebral hypoxia
1 Dementia following multiple infarcts gradually depriving the brain of oxygen.
2 Dementia following prolonged coma, e.g. after carbon monoxide poisoning.
3 Delirium following cerebral haemorrhage.
4 Delirium associated with severe pernicious anaemia.

Dehydration and electrolyte imbalance
1 Delirium due to post operative fluid loss.
2 Delirium in uraemia.

Vitamin deficiency
1 Wernicke's encephalopathy.
2 Alcoholic delirium tremens.

Chronic intoxications
1 Barbiturates.
2 Alcoholic—alcoholic dementia.

Gross cerebral damage
1 Tumour.
2 Chronic inflammation: general paralysis.
3 Head injury causing post-traumatic delirium and dementia.

Investigation of organic syndromes

Physical examination may reveal the cause of delirium or dementia, and may reveal localizing cerebral signs. Commonly, however, physical examination is negative, particularly in cases of dementia, so one employs laboratory and other investigations to clarify the picture. They include:

1 VDRL, RPR, FTA;
2 skull X-ray;
3 E.E.G.;
4 C.S.F. examination;
5 CT brain scan; and
6 cerebral angiography.

Treatment of organic syndromes

General measures

1 *Delirium.* The patient should be nursed in quiet surroundings with minimal interference. Calm doctors and nurses reassure the frightened delirious patient and help to maintain contact with reality however tenuous.

The evening and night time are occasions of heightened overactivity so the patient needs adequate sedation. It is wise to avoid using barbiturates and paraldehyde which may worsen confusion and produce discomfort. Phenothiazine tranquillizers can be given with safety. Diet and fluid should be kept up to the required level and symptomatic treatment with high doses of vitamins is usually given. This should take the form of intravenous parentrovite, 10 ml given 4 hourly for 24 hours, then reduced to 10 ml twice daily intravenously for 24 hours, and then 4 ml intramuscularly daily for 5 days.

2 *Dementia.* The first thing is to find out the extent of the patient's disability so that one can provide him with an environment which is stimulating enough to prevent too rapid deterioration and not too demanding of him. Vitamin B given by mouth is usually given, though the value of this is doubtful.

Occupational therapy and social therapy have a limited though supportive part to play by providing stimulation and preventing social deterioration.

Special measures

In the treatment of delirium and dementia special measures depend on the nature of the underlying disorder if any—for example, adequate antisyphilitic treatment.

Some special examples of organic syndromes

Conditions caused by vitamin deficiency

1 *Korsakov syndrome.* This may be caused by thiamine deficiency, as in alcoholism, or it can be caused by tumour, cerebral trauma and general metabolic disturbance. The clinical picture includes polyneuritis with the following psychiatric symptoms:

gross impairment of recent memory ⎫ This type of organic picture
confabulation   ⎬ is usually called the
disorientation   ⎭ dysmnesic syndrome.

Typically the patient claims recognition of the doctor and describes in detail having met him before, when in fact he has never seen him, or will recount in detail the fancied happenings of the previous day—*confabulation*. Recent memory is so poor that though the examiner may have told the patient his name, he is unable to recollect it a minute later. The onset usually follows delirium tremens. The prognosis for complete recovery is bad.

2 *Wernicke's encephalopathy.* This is caused by thiamine deficiency and is found in severe alcoholism or any state of severe malnutrition. Onset of delirium is often sudden and associated with abnormal pupils, ophthalmoplegia and nystagmus.

3 *Pellagra.* Pellagra is caused by a mixed deficiency of tryptophan and niacin. Psychiatric abnormalities may be diverse, ranging from a neurotic to a psychotic picture, but inevitably a frank organic syndrome emerges. This is usually delirium and, untreated, proceeds to dementia, coma and death.

Cardiovascular disease

1 *Cardiac failure.* Patients in cardiac failure are often subject to bouts of mild confusion or subacute delirium at night. This is caused by relative cerebral hypoxia and responds to further treatment of the cardiac condition.

2 *Multi infarct dementia.* In cerebral arteriosclerosis the onset is earlier than in senile dementia. A typical presentation is episodic with fits, strokes, usually with complete recovery and then a picture of failing memory, concentration and personality change. Stepwise, deterioration is the rule.

3 *Thrombosis of the internal carotid artery.* Occlusion of the internal carotid arteries can give rise to dementia usually complicated by focal cerebral signs. A typical history would include transient losses of power in one or other limbs occurring over a period of months followed by gradual alteration in memory.

Cerebral syphilis or General Paralysis of the Insane (G.P.I.)

Now that syphilis is properly treated in its early stages, the full blown picture of G.P.I. is rarely seen. The first signs of G.P.I. are usually those of sudden personality change, with radical alteration of the patient's previous ethical and moral standards. This is followed by grandiose and extravagant behaviour. After this the picture settles into one of dementia with failing memory and general deterioration. The affective state is usually one of flat euphoria. Spastic paralysis, pupillary abnormalities and physical deterioration are late manifestations.

Syndromes following head injury

Dementia can follow severe head injury, as can fits which are a common sequel of head injury of whatever severity.

Traumatic dementia usually follows extensive destruction of brain tissue. States of delirium with complete recovery can also follow severe head injury.

The term *post-contusional syndrome* is usually applied to a constellation of mild chronic symptoms including headache, dizziness and general feelings of weakness and inability to concentrate. This syndrome is regarded as being constitutionally determined and released by injury. Post-contusional syndromes can present difficult problems in management. In general it is advisable for patients to return to normal life and work as soon as reasonably possible since it has been found that convalescence prolonged unnecessarily delays rehabilitation and fixes neurotic symptoms.

The morale of patients is always improved by confident management, maximum reassurance and vigorous rehabilitation.

Other dementias

1   *Alzheimer's disease* (senile dementia, Alzheimer type) (SDAT)
The original description of Alzheimer's disease was of a pre-senile dementia, but it has for some time been realized that the symptoms and pathology found in Alzheimer's pre-senile dementia and 'senile dementia' are similar, so that now it is customary to refer to this type of dementia—the most common of all—as Alzheimer's disease and when it occurs in the older age groups as senile dementia (Alzheimer type).

Commonly the first manifestations of SDAT are exaggeration of the basic changes of ageing, namely increased rigidity of thinking, greater egocentricity, lessened emotional control. These exaggerations may precede the appearance of frank evidence of dementia, while not for many years, inevitably though, memory impairment, poor concentration and impaired performance show themselves, while the individual's social behaviour becomes less tolerable. Important findings to look for include apraxia, aphasia, and agraphia which are inevitable accompaniments of the disorder. Neglect of the self, appearance and so on become more marked, and the individual enters a decline of all his mental powers until he ends up as an empty shell of his former self, incontinent, helpless, incapable of grasping what is going on around him.

In Alzheimer's disease the frontal and temporal regions of the brain are most commonly affected with severe fall-out in the hippocampal region.

On the other hand, multi infarct dementia related to cerebral atherosclerosis is a less gradual process and shows a step-wise deterioration in mental function. The possibility of pseudo dementia should never be overlooked. In this, in the elderly person, the most common cause is an unrecognized depressive state which usually responds very well to antidepressant treatment.

2 *Pre-senile dementia*
Pre-senile dementia then is an unhelpful term and not now so widely used since it now seems that Alzheimer's disease can occur in the 'pre-senile' and 'senile' stage of life.

3 *Pick's disease*
In this condition cerebral atrophy is mainly confined to the frontal and parietal areas, so that commonly its presentation is as a frontal lobe syndrome with impaired moral standards. This fades into a clinical picture of dementia.

4 *Huntington's chorea*
This is a genetically determined form of dementia. The inheritance is caused by dominant genes. The manifestations of Huntington's chorea are choreiform movements and altered mental states leading inevitably to dementia. A wide range of psychiatric symptomatology may be seen before dementia becomes evident, although the most commonly found psychoses are paranoid in type. Suicide, alcoholism and personality disorders are common in Huntington families.

Psychiatric aspects of epilepsy

The fact is often overlooked that being epileptic is an extremely frightening and threatening experience. The knowledge that one may suddenly without warning have total loss of consciousness is an extremely distressing one for patient and family alike. For this reason the epileptic patient needs, in addition to proper anticonvulsant therapy, sensible support and guidance so that he or she may be enabled to live as normal a life as possible without 'wrapping the patient in cotton wool' which can easily happen with epileptic children. The important special psychiatric aspects of epilepsy concern temporal lobe epilepsy and epileptic psychoses. In temporal lobe epilepsy episodic mood disturbances or outbursts of rage may often be associated with the epileptic discharge and accompanied by appropriate E.E.G. changes. Sometimes T.L.E. may pass unrecognized because the emotional disturbance, whether it is rage, ecstasy or perceptual disturbance, somehow overshadows the seizure-related aspect of the disorder. It should always be considered, when presented with a patient who has an episodic type of behaviour disturbance or mood change.

The association of epilepsy with psychosis is an interesting one. For some time it was thought that there was a negative correlation between schizophrenia and epilepsy. In fact, this is not true. There is a definite association between epilepsy and schizophreniform psychoses and the current view is that these are symptomatic psychoses, i.e. psychoses which originate in the epileptic process and are not independent of it. There is a high correlation between temporal lobe epilepsy and the development of epileptic psychoses.

In the past, personality changes were described in long standing, poorly controlled epileptic patients. The changes noted included tendencies towards rigidity, seclusiveness and rather difficult behaviour. These changes are uncommon and were probably related to prolonged stay in institutions plus the effects of taking excessive medication. Perhaps the only association between epilepsy and personality change is an apparent association, at least, between temporal lobe epilepsy and personality disorder.

Syndromes associated with cerebral tumour

The common modes of presentation of cerebral tumour are:
1 epilepsy;
2 signs of raised intracranial pressure, e.g. headache, papilloedema, nausea, vertigo;

3   manifestations of local or generalized brain damage, e.g. dysphasia, apraxia, dementia, paresis.

However, it is not uncommon for tumours to present with apparently 'pure' psychiatric symptoms. Even more misleading can be the occurrence of tumour in a patient with long standing neurotic complaints. In either instance if the doctor is not alert the diagnosis will be missed until signs of gross damage appear.

Probably about 50% of patients with cerebral tumour present in this way, i.e. with psychiatric symptomatology. This places a critical diagnostic burden on anyone evaluating such symptoms, particularly in children and in patients of middle age who are most at risk for tumour development.

The following manifestations should always be enquired about most carefully and evaluated:

1   subtle, insidious personality change
2   deterioration in appearance } point to frontal lobe tumours
3   altered ethical and moral standards
4   recent affective flattening, insouciance and apathy

5   unusual flippancy
6   poor concentration } point to temporal lobe tumours
7   memory impairment
8   hallucinations

9   bouts of sleepiness } point to third ventricle tumours.

REFERENCES

Bleuler M. (1951) Psychiatry of cerebral diseases. *Br. med. J.*, ii, 420, 460, 463.

Hare E. H. (1959) The origin and spread of dementia paralytica. *J. ment. Sci.*, 105, 594.

Keschner M., Bender M. & Strauss I. (1938) Mental symptoms associated with brain tumour. Study of 530 verified cases. *J. Am. Med. Ass.*, 110, 714.

Lishman A. L. (1980) *Organic Psychiatry*. Blackwell Scientific Publications, Oxford.

Lipowski Z. J. (1980) *Delirium—Acute Brain Failure in Man*. Charles C. Thomas, Springfield, Illinois.

Slater E., Beard A. W. & Clitheroe (1963) The schizophrenic-like psychoses of epilepsy. *Br. J. Psychiatry*, 109, 95.

Symonds C. (1962) Concussion and its sequelae. *Lancet*, i, 1.

Wolff H. G. & Curran D. (1935) Nature of delirium and allied states. *Arch. Neurol. Psychiatry*, 331, 175.

CHAPTER 5
NEUROSIS AND PERSONALITY
DISORDER

Introduction

The disease concept in psychiatry is strongest as far as the organic psychoses are concerned. In these disorders, structural brain pathology produces recognizable psychiatric syndromes. The concept is less strong in the case of the functional psychoses, i.e. *schizophrenia* and *manic depressive psychosis*, though evidence of *biochemical disturbance* is impressive. In the case of the neuroses and personality disorders, this concept is at its weakest since these conditions are quantitative differences from the normal, as opposed to specific disorders such as the organic and functional psychoses.

Neurotic depression and anxiety can be triggered off by many causes and are often found in people with vulnerable or abnormal personalities. This means that neurosis and personality disorder are interwoven. Many find it difficult to accept personality disorder as an *illness* because personality disorders do not represent a change in an individual any more than does being ugly or beautiful—so that is how the person is!

The neuroses

Everyone agrees that neurosis is an unsatisfactory and out-of-date term and everyone uses it. Laymen and some doctors use it to encompass self-indulgent failure to pull the self together. In psychiatry many definitions are available: none are perfect.

A general concept of neurosis identifies it as a psychological disorder characterized by:
1   the absence of symptoms such as hallucinations, delusions, thought disorder or intellectual impairment;
2   the presence of anxiety;
3   mild chronic symptoms;
4   preservation of insight; and
5   no change in personality.

As opposed to the psychoses—severe disorders characterized by:
1   manifestations such as hallucinations, delusions, thought disorder and intellectual impairment;
2   severe mood disturbance;
3   poor insight;
4   relative absence of anxiety; and
5   personality change.

The neuroses are common disorders and account for 20–25% of patients attending general practitioners. The neuroses covered here include:
1   anxiety;
2   hysteria;
3   obsessional disorder; and
4   hypochondriasis.

ANXIETY

Anxiety is a universal phenomenon in which the subject experiences a feeling *akin to fear or apprehension* usually accompanied by autonomic disturbances (sympathetic overactivity), of which the following are typical:
1   tachycardia and raised blood pressure;
2   palpitations;
3   dryness of mouth;
4   diarrhoea, epigastric discomfort, nausea;
5   dilated pupils;
6   sweating;
7   frequency of micturition; and
8   headache.

Despite its universality, not all anxiety is pathological. It is useful to distinguish between *healthy* and *morbid* anxiety.

Healthy anxiety is experienced by most people under unaccustomed *stress*—examinations, interviews, etc., being typical examples. It is a normal response to an unusual situation, an *adaptive response* on the part of the organism which prepares him for a task or ordeal requiring further effort and making unusual demands on him.

Morbid anxiety, however, is different; it is an *unadaptive response* and serves no useful purpose, once it is established—quite the opposite in fact! Too often it pervades the mental life of the individual and becomes a rein not a spur. The morbidly anxious patient is soon aware of the *paradoxical nature* of his affliction. Anxiety is experienced both in the presence of, or the absence of what can be seen to be obvious stimuli. The patient knows that his fears are irrational and groundless but this is no help to him as he magnifies, scrutinizes and mulls over the content of his anxiety.

Aetiology

Age

Anxiety is common in adolescence and old age. *Adolescence* can be and often is a time of stress and turmoil. Young people are subject to all sorts of pressures at this time of their lives. Normal adolescent development is a period during which strong emotions are easily aroused—emotions which the subject finds hard to channel. He is at an 'in between' stage of life where he is accorded neither adult nor childish status. He is often oversensitive and prickly, particularly about his appearance which is more often than not gauche and pimply. It is hardly surprising then that emergent sexuality is tantalized by advertisements extolling the virtues of flawless skin or correct bust size. The adolescent is full of doubts about himself, Will he get a job, the right sort of job? Will he get into a university? Is he going to be socially, sexually and in every other way competent when put to the test? All these sorts of questions are in his mind and it seems to him that everyone offers conflicting advice. In this setting he may develop *anxiety symptoms,* usually of an acute sort.

Often the anxiety symptoms of the adolescent may find their most extreme expression in a near psychotic breakdown—sometimes mistakenly diagnosed as schizophrenia—which has been called the *adolescent crisis of identity.* This syndrome is really what the name suggests, a state in which the youngster becomes so uncertain of himself and his role that he breaks down into an overwhelming state of anxious uncertainty where contact with reality may apparently be lost. A good fictional description of this is to be found in the novel *Catcher in the Rye* by J. D. Salinger.

The adolescent crisis of identity usually responds well to straight-forward and sympathetic management. It is important that such patients are not mistakenly *labelled* as schizophrenic; on the other hand it has to be remembered that schizophrenia is a state which can and does begin in adolescence. But in schizophrenia the evidence for a more profound process should be sought for, personality change, thought disorder, etc. (see Schizophrenia, p. 29.)

Sources of anxiety in adolescence then are common; they may be personal, social or cultural. The symptom itself needs investigation and treatment since adolescence is a time of change and maturation. Sensible handling in adolescence may help the individual avoid chronicity of symptoms and the carry over of unresolved adolescent problems in adult life.

Elderly people readily beome anxious when the orderly routine of their life is threatened. Loneliness and the fear of death are also important causes of anxiety in old age. Often the anxieties of the elderly may be too readily dismissed as if they were of little significance because the patient is *old*. As if old age were necessarily a sort of laissez passer to wretchedness which it need not be though too often is.

Constitution

Some people are, by nature, more anxious than others. From early years and throughout their lives they are insecure, timid, and emotionally unstable. Their fears are easily aroused and they are over fussy about their health—tending readily towards hypochondriasis. Their *work records* are *poor,* and they show a *low level* of *drive, energy, ambition* and *persistence.* This combination of traits is regarded as evidence of *constitutional neuroticism* and the evidence for its existence has been convincingly demonstrated (Slater, Rees and Eysenck). Neuroticism correlates highly with physique, vasomotor instability and a background of poor general health.

Learning

There is much experimental evidence to suggest that where anxiety is linked to *specific stressors* (cats, open spaces etc.) the *phobia* as it is called, is a learned phenomenon, i.e. has been developed by a process of simple conditioning and is subject to the same laws (generalization, inhibition, extinction etc.). This has been exploited therapeutically by using processes of *deconditioning* to extinguish *phobias* (see Treatment, p. 60).

Clinical manifestations

In addition to experiencing the specific manifestations described at the beginning of this section, anxious patients often complain of feelings of *tension*, or of difficulty in *concentrating.* Tension manifests itself not only by a 'feeling of being strung up' but also by heaviness or pains in the limbs.

Associated *mood change of depressive type* is very commonly associated with anxiety—in fact a state of anxiety in pure culture is extremely rare—sooner or later depression appears.

Other bodily accompaniments of anxiety include decreased libido and impotence. Sleep is poor—typically the patient finds it hard to get off to sleep and may experience broken sleep throughout the night when he will tend to wake and lie awake worrying about his fears.

Anxiety states may present to the doctor in a wide range of symptoms involving almost every system of the body: The cardiologist may be consulted about palpitations; the chest physician about difficulty in breathing; the gastro-enterologist about dyspepsia and the neurologist about weakness and headaches. So, that the bodily manifestations of anxiety are likely to be those of which the patient complains—since they are what make him feel unwell. While careful investigation is a part of all medical care it has to be realized that in the treatment of the patient with anxiety that investigation carried to excess may reinforce the disorder. So that the doctor has to strike a balance between overinvestigation and inadequate reassurance and underinvestigation with overconfident reassurance.

Diagnosis

Simple states of anxiety uncomplicated by depression are uncommon—most anxious patients have some depressive mood change. Anxiety may be prominent in the onset of a depressive illness. It is also not uncommon to find anxiety in the early stages of schizophrenia. Before deciding that a patient is suffering from simple anxiety one has to exclude:
1   depression, and
2   schizophrenia.

However episodic attacks which can be confused with anxiety can be caused by:
1   temporal lobe epilepsy;
2   adrenalin secreting tumours; and
3   hypoglycaemia.

Treatment

Physical

1 *Tranquillizers*

Formerly the barbiturates were commonly used in the treatment of anxiety symptoms but unhappily because of their overprescription by an irresponsible minority of doctors for an irresponsible minority of patients, they have lost their previously impeccable credentials. We may add to this the fact that barbiturates are dangerous drugs from the overdose and dependency point of view and also because of their facility for inducing liver microenzymes, they can considerably interfere with the activity of other drugs that the patient may be taking. So for these reasons, despite their effectiveness as relievers of anxiety, they have been gradually replaced by benzodiazepine tranquillizers.

The main tranquillizers used include:

Chlordiazepoxide (Librium)	up to 60 mg daily
Diazepam (Valium)	up to 60 mg daily
Oxazepam (Serenid)	up to 90 mg daily
Lorazepam (Ativan)	up to 2 mg t.i.d.

Admittedly the tranquillizers or anxiolytic drugs are strictly speaking tranquilosedative and have a limited abuse potential, but it is nowhere so great as that of barbiturates. Excessive doses of benzodiazepines can produce states of chronic intoxication with drowsiness, dysarthria and ataxia and also withdrawal fits if larger doses are stopped suddenly.

2 *Beta-adrenergic blocking agents*

This is covered more fully in Chapter 12. The beta-adrenergic receptor blocking drugs are the newest drugs used in the treatment of anxiety and have an increasing place in the management of anxious patients, particularly those who have somatic manifestations of anxiety, tremor, palpitations, sweating, etc.

Psychological

Psychological treatment of anxiety is of two sorts: psychotherapy, and behaviour therapy.

1 *Psychotherapy*

Psychotherapy aims to relieve anxiety by discovering causes in the patient's unconscious mental life, by solving problems and resolving conflict. There are many schools of psychotherapy (e.g. Freudian and Jungian), but all subscribe to the belief that behaviour is controlled by unconscious forces and emotion rather than by reason.

The simplest form of psychotherapy is *supportive*. In this the doctor listens and permits the patient to ventilate his feelings and arrive at solutions of problems without guidance or interpretation. The role of the doctor is to provide unbiased sympathy and encouragement.

Analytic psychotherapy aims at exploration of the unconscious. It is necessarily a lengthy process. The most suitable subjects are people with above average intelligence and good verbal ability. The two most widely known schools of analytic psychotherapy are Freudian and Jungian analysis. All psychotherapeutic methods acknowledge the fundamental importance of the relationship that exists between patient and doctor in psychotherapy. This relationship can vary from one extreme to another as the patient invests the doctor with every sort of emotion. The trained psychotherapist accepts this relationship and handles it as part of the therapeutic process. The patient transfers to the doctor, emotions which previously he had experienced about key figures in his personality development. This is called 'the transference'.

2 *Behaviour therapy*

When anxiety is linked to specific stresses (e.g. cats, heights, open spaces) and only triggered off by these, it is called *phobic anxiety*. These phobias may be single or multiple.

In recent years, psychologists studying theories of learning have pointed out that phobias are probably the result of maladaptive learning, i.e. the patient has become conditioned to experience anxiety at the sight or sound of a given object. They have reasoned from this that the phobias could be cured by a deconditioning process which desensitizes the patient from the cause of the attacks. This has the advantage of being based on a rational theoretical basis. The most obvious drawback appears to be that its usefulness is limited by the fact that it is only applicable to patients with isolated phobias.

Behaviour therapy has been criticized for the failure to take into account the existence of a therapeutic relationship between doctor and patient and its consequent effects in altering the course of the patient's illness. However, more careful evaluation of behaviour therapeutic methods has shown that this need not necessarily be the case.

In general, it may be said that the term behaviour therapy is applied to a variety of psychiatric treatment in which use is made of the principles of behavioural sciences in re-educating a patient away from abnormal behaviour.

The theoretical basis runs counter to a dynamic basis in that it rejects the supposed importance of unconscious processes and conflict, stressing rather the importance of symptoms as learnt manifestations of a neurotic disorder.

The beginning of behaviour therapy occurred in the early 1950s when Professor H. J. Eysenck and colleagues in the Institute of Psychiatry in London made serious criticisms of the value of conventional psychotherapy and suggested in its stead the use of behaviour therapy a treatment in which learnt neurotic responses would be replaced using learning and deconditioning techniques.

Typical methods of behaviour therapy include: (a) conditioned avoidance; (b) reciprocal inhibition: (c) desensitization; (d) flooding; and (e) modelling.

(a) *Conditioned avoidance.* In these techniques the behaviour to be extinguished—e.g. alcoholism, sexual deviation, is linked to an aversive stimulus such as apomorphine causing nausea thus producing in the subject a state of conditioned aversion.

(b) *Reciprocal inhibition.* This technique is based on the finding that some human behaviours are mutually exclusive, e.g. relaxation and tension. In practice use is made of this finding by endeavouring to replace an unwanted response by one which is incompatible with it. In time the subject responds with relaxation to situations which have previously caused fear.

(c) *Desensitization.* Here the subject learns to avoid responding to noxious stimuli by being exposed to the stimuli at such minimal levels that little or no unpleasant response occurs. In this way his tolerance to the stimuli improves and the response is lost.

(d) *Flooding.* A newer technique in behaviour therapy is 'flooding' or 'implosion' in which the patient is not desensitized from the dreaded stimulus but brought face to face with it until the anxiety fades. It sounds terrible but it works!

(e) *Modelling.* In this the phobic patient learns to overcome the feared stimulus by witnessing a therapist dealing with it. For instance, if the patient had a phobia of dogs, the patient would learn to model his behaviour on a therapist who introduced the patient into a room where there was a dog present and who was able to handle the dog, etc. without displaying any evidence of anxiety. In fact, modelling has become one of the most frequently used types of behaviour therapy.

HYSTERIA

The word hysteria is used in at least four ways:

1   To describe a variety of abnormal personality, *hysterical personality*.

2   To describe certain disorders, *hysterical disorder (conversion hysteria)*, in which there is loss of function without organic damage. These disorders are induced by stress and the patient is unconscious of the mechanism.

3   To describe unconscious exaggeration of organic disease, so called *'hysterical overlay'* or 'hysterical exaggeration'.

4   To describe states of mind in which an individual becomes 'out of control', 'beside herself'. This is a lay use of the term, but used surprisingly frequently by doctors.

Hysterical personality (histrionic personality)

The term hysterical personality has been used to describe a personality type, characterized by a tendency towards histrionic behaviour. Such individuals show the following traits: (a) affective immaturity often allied to an appearance of physical immaturity; (b) egocentricity allied to a remarkable capacity for self deception; (c) histrionic behaviour. (To the hysteric the world is either hell or heaven. Extremes of feeling easily aroused and as easily dissipated are commonplace. This is reflected in their appearance in striking fashion. At one moment the patient is an ashen-faced, weeping wreck threatening suicide, disrupting the whole atmosphere of the ward—hours later or less, she is the most vivacious and sought after partner at the hospital dance); and (d) Inability to tolerate or maintain interpersonal relationships of any depth.

Of course the hysteric possesses these traits to an excessive degree—they are common enough in normal people. Under certain circum-stances the hysterical personality can be an asset, e.g. in the theatre.

Hysterical disorders (conversion hysteria)

In hysterical disorders there is loss of function without organic damage. This arises as a result of stress usually in a susceptible person but can occur in otherwise normal individuals in face of overwhelming stress (e.g. disasters, wartime, etc.)

The lost function protects the patient from further harm. Is the illness simulated, it may be asked. The answer is, Yes, but the patient is wholly or partly unaware of this.

Hysterical disorders are diverse. Most commonly they affect higher functions and the central nervous system producing amnaesia, paralysis, sensory loss etc. Hysteria can also produce pseudo dementia in which the patient develops an apparent psychotic state. The signs of 'psychosis' confirm to the layman's idea of madness, e.g. when asked how many legs has a cow a patient might answer 'five'. Pains can be hysterical in origin. When this is so it is a common error to suppose that the patient is therefore not experiencing discomfort but is feigning. As so little is known about the mechanism of pain there seems no justification for this belief. It is wiser to acknowledge that the patient is in pain and try and discover the cause. Pain is pain whether hysterical or not, and the label hysterical should not be allowed to cause patients to be subjected to the sort of hostile treatment that they may provoke by their admittedly often demanding and rather ruthless behaviour.

Aetiology

1 The role of the hysterical personality has been mentioned. There is strong evidence to support the belief that genetic factors are important in this.
2 It is likely too that upbringing can reinforce already dominant hysterical traits. The doting parent who accedes to every whim of an unstable egocentric child is probably doing this unwittingly.
3 *Brain damage, mental subnormality and chronic psychosis* all predispose to hysteria by lowering higher control and integration.
4 Hysterical disorders are danger signals. The undiagnosed depressive or the incipient schizophrene who finds his inner life mysteriously disrupted—both may develop hysterical symptoms as an unconscious call for help.
5 The manifestations of hysteria conform to: (a) the patient's notion of illness, thus sensory loss is of 'glove' or 'stocking' distribution; and (b) ideas of disease implanted in the patient's mind by others either by suggestion or example. Doctors can suggest the former and other patients the latter by their own symptoms.
6 The psychodynamic explanation of hysterical disorder is that the failure in function always arises as a result of unconscious conflict or buried psychic trauma which threaten the individual's integrity to such an extent that he responds by switching off a function thus making it unnecessary to continue in the stressful situation as he is now ill and can opt out of the situation demanding his attention. This switching off is referred to as dissociation.

Diagnosis

Since hysteria can mimic so many other illnesses the differential diagnosis is limitless. The diagnosis should be made on positive and not negative grounds; it is not good enough to investigate a patient's complaints and, having found no abnormality, fall back on hysteria as a convenient dumping ground.

One must have adequate reasons for making the diagnosis, so that one can look at the patient's history and life situation and see with certainty that a hysterical disorder is the inevitable outcome of all that has gone before.

Hysteria is a diagnosis that is often made lightly by the inexperienced, purely on the basis of a few negative results.

Treatment

Hysterical personality disorder

Such patients usually make brief dramatic appearances in hospital following suicidal gestures, marital strife or any acute stress that is too much for their level of tolerance. Mood disturbances may be prominent but rarely sustained.

Tranquillizing drugs may be needed to calm the patient in a period of acute crisis. The object should be to make the period of hospital stay as short as possible to tide the patient over the crisis.

After this, treatment either consists of: (a) simple supportive therapy, or (b) prolonged psychotherapy aimed at helping the patient towards insight and a higher level of emotional maturity.

Hysterical disorder (conversion hysteria)

1 *General measures.* It is important to treat the patient actively, i.e. to do everything possible that will help to convince him that total function will return. At the same time one has to avoid focusing too much on the symptom and reinforcing it in the patient's mind.

This can be done fairly easily as long as doctors and nurses approach the patient as a team and with full knowledge of each other's roles. Difference of opinion and uncertainty feed hysteria. The patient, sensing differing attitudes, questions different people, gets different answers and his symptoms intensify and proliferate.

2 *Abreaction.* Freud used this term to describe the re-living of emotionally charged experiences said to have caused hysterical breakdown. Abreaction has a place in the treatment of hysteria but is most successful in the acute disorder, i.e. immediately following some traumatic experience.

Abreaction is encouraged in a state of altered consciousness—usually brought about by giving intravenous sodium amytal (250–500 mg). In theory the patient regains the lost function once he has ventilated the pent-up feeling that surrounds the traumatic scene.

3 *Psychotherapy.* The alternatives are: (a) supportive therapy, or (b) commencing exploratory psychotherapy with the object of helping the patient to understand the nature of his illness and how it relates to his life situation. This means embarking on fairly prolonged psychotherapy.

OBSESSIONAL DISORDERS

Obsessions and compulsions are similar though not identical psychological manifestations. Their similarity lies in the fact that they are both experienced against an inner feeling of resistance. Obsessions are contents of consciousness, i.e. ideas or thoughts which the patient has and which he tries to push away. Sometimes they develop into acts, utterances or rituals, and become repetitive, in which case they are called compulsions. In practice they are described collectively by the term obsessive compulsive phenomena.

Aetiology

Normal development

Everyone has experienced the 'tune that keeps running through the head', or the rituals practised in childhood, e.g. walking on paving stones avoiding the lines. These are part of normal life and development and resemble obsessive compulsive phenomena. Children often use these rituals in a magical way to defend themselves from fancied harm. It has been suggested that rituals are used in a similar way in obsessional illness.

Personality type

Some people are from their early years overmeticulous and unduly scrupulous. They show excessive concern for order and tidiness in dress and in their surroundings. Their talk is precise, even pedantic, while their outlook is excessively moral and rigid. They tend to be indecisive, vacillatory and hypochondriacal. Their indecisiveness makes them good subordinates but poor leaders. They lack imagination or creative ability, and humour, when present, is of an arid donnish sort. These sort of traits constitute the *obsessional personality*. If such people become psychologically ill, they develop obsessional symptoms. When such individuals develop say a depressive state, their illness tends to be very much coloured by their personality so that they often present with an interminable kind of pedantic hypochondriacal talk which may mask the depressive mood change which becomes more apparent as the interview proceeds.

Relation to brain damage

1   Obsessional symptoms are definitely associated with the personality changes following encephalitis lethargica.
2   The brain damaged patient often develops obsessional tidiness, 'organic orderliness'. This can be seen as the way in which a progressively handicapped individual attempts to impose order on an environment that is becoming too much for him.

Manifestations

Obsessional symptoms tend to focus on daily activities such as eating, dressing, washing and defaecation—a patient complained that she was unable to eat as she spent hours removing solid particles from food matter. Another patient never finished her housework as she felt obliged to repeat the washing-up time and time again. A patient could not get to work on time as he was delayed by elaborate rituals surrounding his morning defaecation.

Usually the patient seeks medical advice because the symptom has *got out of hand*. It has usually been present for some time but recently become troublesome.

Mood change of a depressive sort is a common association, obsessions get worse with depression and vice versa, so a vicious circle is set up.

Anguish, anxiety and tension are frequent accompaniments. The obsessional's tendency to self-criticism is unduly exaggerated. He describes the symptoms of his illness in strongly self-condemnatory terms, apparently quite failing to see them as illness at all, when any of his friends etc., quite easily recognize that he is unwell.

Differential diagnosis

The pure obsessional is often hard to distinguish from a depressive illness with obsessional features since depression usually accompanies the former. This history, however, should be helpful.

Schizophrenia may present as an obsessional illness, or obsessional features may complicate it. This can present a tricky diagnostic problem. Obsessions associated with schizophrenia tend to be rather bizarre.

Treatment

Psychotherapy

Analytic psychotherapy of obsessional illness aims at discovering the symbolic meaning of the phenomena, for the psychoanalytic view of obsessional illness is that it results from overactivity of the superego which defends the ego against overwhelming anxiety by magical rituals. In practice obsessionals do not respond particularly well to psychotherapy, their pedantry and excessive concern with detail cause them to become enmeshed in the therapeutic process and brought to a halt.

Supportive therapy however can help the patient to ventilate pent up feelings about his rituals and afford him some relief of anxiety and tension.

Medication

1   Tranquillizers can be useful in reducing anxiety. The most commonly used include Diazepam, Chlordiazepoxide, and Oxazepam.
2   Antidepressant drugs should always be tried whenever there is any evidence of depression.

Physical treatment

1   E.C.T. is useful in the presence of depression.
2   Psychosurgery is used in the treatment of chronic severe obsessional disorder accompanied by persistent tension and misery.

Natural history and prognosis

Obsessional illnesses show phases of remission and exacerbation (Pollitt 1960) so that the long-term outlook is not so gloomy as is sometimes feared. Nevertheless the illness can be crippling. It is useful to use social criteria in assessing the degree of handicap, e.g. one should try and find out how long per day the patient spends on his rituals; do they prevent him from working or is he late for work etc.?

The presence of depression of any degree makes the outlook better.

HYPOCHONDRIASIS

Preoccupation with fancied bodily illness is a persistent and trouble-some experience which can cause misery, prolonged and unnecessary investigation and mounting impatience in the doctor confronted with the querulous demands of the hypochondriac. For convenience it is classified with the neuroses—the majority of hypochondriacs are neurotic but at the same time it should be conceded that hypochondriasis can be delusional. The classification of hypochondriasis is contentious—the main point being is there such a thing as 'essential hypochondriasis'. In general hypochondriasis may colour:
1   neurotic depression,
2   anxiety,
3   obsessional disorder,
4   hysteria,
and bizarre hypochondriasis can occur in schizophrenia. There is a residue of hypochondriacal people who do not fit into this classification and who go through life preoccupied with their health—a history of minor ailments in childhood grossly overtreated is common.

Managment of the hypochondriacal patient includes:
1   Vigorous treatment of anxiety or depression,
2   Calling a halt to unnecessary investigation,
3   Individual supportive therapy by the same physician. Passing the patient from one doctor to another only makes matters worse,
4   Finally doctors should recognize that hypochondriasis is easily fostered in a pill-oriented age.

ABNORMAL PERSONALITY AND PSYCHOPATHY

Many people behave abnormally from their earliest years. This abnormality can show itself in antisocial acts, drug addiction, social inadequacy, undue vulnerability or in eccentricity of one sort or another. It is part of their constitution rather than an acquired illness and for this reason is ascribed to their having *abnormal personalities.*

PERSONALITY—NORMAL AND ABNORMAL

Personality is the sum of many different varying characteristics, intellectual, affective and physical, to name only a few, which gives to each person both an individuality and a resemblance to his fellows. These characteristics are present to some degree in everyone, so that to speak of *normal* and *abnormal* personality is not to postulate endpoints separating the two categories, but rather to define an individual's personality as lying somewhere along a curve of normal distribution. In this way the abnormals are those who deviate markedly from the average and the normals are the bulk of the population. This method of considering personality has the great advantage of being *experimentally* valuable. Investigators can then go further and attempt to establish the psychological correlates of given personality characteristics. Much valuable work of this sort has already been carried out. The psychiatric approach to the study of *abnormal personalities* has in the main been a clinical one and has not been made easy to follow by the use of the term *psychopath.*

In general, psychiatrists have tended to call psychopaths those patients with abnormal personalities, but this is not universally so. The two concepts of psychopathy and personality disorder were most succinctly united by Schneider (1958) who defined psychopaths as *those abnormal personalities who suffer from their abnormality or cause society to suffer.* This definition is the one used in this book. It has one very important advantage, namely that it recognizes that someone can have an abnormal personality without being regarded in some way as ill or antisocial, i.e. distinguishes between 'pathological' and 'non-pathological' abnormal personalities. This is important because the term psychopath has come to be regarded in Anglo-American circles anyway, almost as a term of abuse.

Unfortunately the picture (in England and Wales) has been made more complicated by the Mental Health Act of 1959, in which the definition of psychopathic disorder stresses irresponsible or antisocial conduct.

Psychiatrists have classified psychopaths in two main ways; first by naming groups whose personality disorder resembles a clinical syndrome, e.g. schizoid psychopath, hysterical psychopath and secondly, by naming groups whose personality disorder resembles a clinical syndrome, e.g. inadequate psychopath, aggressive psychopath.

Variations of abnormal personalities

Non-pathological

Many people of undoubted genius fall into this category. Some authorities would call them psychopaths but there seems no justification for this.

Pathological (= Psychopaths)

The abnormalities which cause symptoms include
neuroticism
instability
lability of mood $\Big\}$ may lead to admission to hospital.
abuse of drugs

The abnormalities which offend society include
suicidal gestures
antisocial behaviour—recidivism
lack of foresight leading to
   gratification of any need $\Big\}$ may lead to hospital,
explosive behaviour   or more commonly to prison.
sexual perversions
social inadequacy
inability to maintain stable
   interpersonal relationships

    The striking feature of so many psychopaths is their *remarkable degree of immaturity* of personality development. They react to the whim of the moment in much the same way as does a small child who has tantrums if his wishes are not gratified immediately. The same sort of thing leads them into crimes which can have disastrous consequences.

Treatment

There is no treatment which can transform someone's personality, on the other hand prolonged psychotherapy can be helpful to the intelligent psychopath—it is a way of focusing on his problems whilst he forms a relationship with the therapist.

Social rehabilitation

Social rehabilitation of the antisocial psychopath is attempted by group therapy in special communities (therapeutic community). In these, the traditional hierarchical hospital structure is done away with since psychopaths do not do well in such a situation. Instead the approach to the patient acknowledges the importance of social forces and of the community as a whole in influencing behaviour. The unit is run on democratic rather than autocratic lines and the whole community of patients and staff share the responsibility for determining the behaviours that they can tolerate (Rapaport 1960). There is growing evidence to show that psychopaths do well in such units.

Medication

1   Tranquillizers and sedatives may be used in helping psychopaths through crises but there is no justification for routine long-term medication except in the case of aggressive psychopaths who can be kept calm with phenothiazines.
2   Antidepressant drugs may be used when sustained depression is encountered.

REFERENCES

Beech H. R. (1974) *Obsessional States.* Methuen, London.
Curran D. & Mallinson P. (1944) Psychopathic personality. *J. ment. Sci.,* **90,** 266.
Freud S. (1936) *The Problem of Anxiety.* Norton, New York.
Freud S. (1959) Mourning and melancholia. In *Collected Papers,* vol. 4. Basic Books, New York.
Grimshaw L. (1965) The outcome of obsessional disorder; a follow up study of 100 cases. *Br. J. Psychiatry,* **111,** 1051.
Guze S. B. (1975) The validity and significance of the clinical diagnosis of hysteria (Briquet's Syndrome). *Am. J. Psychiatry,* **132,** 138.
Henderson D. K. (1939) *Psychopathic States.* Norton, New York.
Horney K. (1937) *The Neurotic Personality of Our Time.* Norton, New York.
Klein M. (1950) *Contributions to Psycho Analysis.* Hogarth, London.
Kringlen E. (1965) Obsessional neurotics—a long term follow up. *Br. J. Psychiatry,* **111,** 709.
Lewis A. J. (1935) Problems of obsessional illness. *Proc. Roy. Soc. Med.,* **29,** 325.
Lewis A. (1974) Psychopathic personality: a most elusive category. *Psychol. Med.,* **4,** 133.
Lewis A. (1975) The survival of hysteria. *Psychol. Med.,* **5,** 9.

Ljundberg (1957) Hysteria, a genetic and prognostic survey. *Acta Psychiat. Neurol. Scand.*, **112**, suppl., 22.

Mai F. M. & Merskey H. (1980) Briquet's treatise on hysteria—a synopsis and commentary. *Arch. Gen. Psychiatry*, **37**, 1401.

Marks I. M. (1969) *Fears and Phobias.* Heinemann, London.

Marks I. M. (1973) Research in neurosis: a selective review. 1. Causes and courses. *Psychol Med.*, **3**, 436.

Meyer V. & Crisp A. H. (1966) Some problems in behaviour therapy. *Br. J. Psychiatry*, **112**, 367.

Pollitt J. (1960) Natural history studies in mental illness. *J. ment. Sci.*, **106**, 442.

Pollitt J. (1969) Obsessional states. *Br. J. Hosp. Med.*, **5**, 1146.

Rees L. (1950) Body size, personality and neurosis. *J. ment. Sci.*, **96**, 168.

Rees L. & Eysenck H. J. (1945) A factorial study of some morphological and psychological aspects of human constitution. *J. ment. Sci.*, **91**, 8.

Slater E. (1943) The neurotic constitution. *J. Neurol. Psychiatry*, **6**, 1.

Scott P. D. (1960) The treatment of psychopaths. *Br. med. J.*, i, 1641.

Schneider K. (1958) *Psychopathic Personalities.* Cassell, London.

Slater E. (1965) Diagnosis of hysteria. *Br. med. J.*, i, 1395.

CHAPTER 6
ALCOHOLISM AND DRUG DEPENDENCE

Introduction

Alcoholism is a serious social problem in the U.K. At least 1 in 20 of the population is a problem drinker. The cost is enormous, in 1977 the financial loss in industrial output through alcoholism was around £500 000 000 and the cost to Health and Social Services around £52 000 000. The recognition of alcohol-related problems is now a matter of medical and social urgency of which all doctors should be aware—particularly in general practice since too many problem drinkers pass unrecognized by too many doctors.

Definition

The term alcoholism, never easily defined, has now been replaced by alcohol-dependence and problem drinking, though the W.H.O. retains the word alcoholism to cover dependence and problem drinking. Problem drinking is alcohol consumption which leads to physical, psychological or social problems, or all three. Alcoholics never recognize themselves as being 'alcoholics' but accept the term 'problem drinker'. Thus 'alcoholism' is retained as a *generic* term. Problem drinking should be simply recognized because it is dose related. This is something that has been clarified in recent years. A sound rule is that anyone who drinks more than five pints of beer a day, or its equivalent in wine or spirits, is a problem drinker and is in danger of developing complications, and becoming alcohol dependent. As consumption rises the individual will develop withdrawal symptoms, both physical and psychological. Physical dependence on alcohol is a dose-related syndrome in which withdrawal symptoms appear within 12 hours of the last drink. The patient sweats profusely, develops tremor, cardiac arrhythmia, retching and vomiting, and may have withdrawal fits. He learns to allay these symptoms by drinking.

Chapter 6

Incidence

The incidence of alcohol-related problems is hard to estimate but the figure of one in twenty of the population in the U.K. seems definite. For this reason, early recognition of a destructive process which can destroy health, personal relationships, professional life and prospects, is very important. A conservative estimate is 2 000 000 problem drinkers in the U.K. Twenty-five per cent of patients in general hospitals have alcohol related pathology.

Aetiology

The most important fact of aetiology is the dose level. The more alcohol a person consumes the more damage is done. A family history of alcoholism is an important factor—alcoholics tend to have alcoholic fathers. A small percentage of alcoholics, probably less than 10%, are so-called 'symptomatic alcoholics' who are using alcohol as a form of self medication against feelings of anxiety and/or depression, themselves made worse by the alcohol. It should be emphasized that alcoholic patients, however, are a heterogeneous group of individuals damaged by a toxin. Psychological stereotypes of 'alcoholic personalities' are misleading and unhelpful. This is not to say that people do not use alcohol to relieve neurotic anxiety or escape from problems in living, in many cases they do, but social factors are highly relevant. The use of alcohol as a social lubricant in business, the tolerance of public drunkeness and heavy drinking, are all factors which encourage people not to control their drinking. Certain occupations are highly at risk, these include barmen, merchant sailors, members of the armed forces and the entertainment industry, and particularly doctors.

Clinical manifestations

Introduction

There is a pattern in the history of problem drinking which can at least aid in the diagnosis and the following features are found to be signs that drinking is getting out of control:
1 gulping;
2 taking extra drinks before parties;
3 drinking on the way home;

4   drinking during the day;
5   lying about one's consumption of alcohol;
6   avoiding the topic of alcohol in conversation;
7   concealing alcohol on the person;
8   carrying drink to work;
9   taking liveners on rising; and
10 amnesic gaps.

The incipient alcoholic passes through a stage of habitual excessive drinking bouts till he is drinking all the time.

The full-blown clinical picture may be easily recognized by the familiar picture of the red-faced, obese, probably bronchitic, toper, moving from saloon bar joviality to maudlin tears or uncontrolled anger with easy rapidity.

Recognition and diagnosis

The recognition of the alcoholic patient consists in looking at the total picture of the patient and being on the look-out for physical complications. Often the patient presents with these and does not mention his drinking history at all. In all cases, a useful tactic is to take a complete history of the patient's drinking habits during a typical 24 hours. This is more revealing than merely asking how much the patient drinks. A raised MCV and raised gamma glutamyl transferase level are excellent screening tests. Physical complications of chronic alcoholism include:

1   nausea;
2   gastritis;
3   diarrhoea;
4   hepatic cirrhosis, liver failure, portal systemic encepalopathy;
5   piles;
6   pancreatitis;
7   bronchitis;
8   pulmonary tuberculosis;
9   peripheral neuritis;
10 macrocytic anaemia;
11 hypertension and coronary heart disease;
12 late onset epilepsy;
13 fetal alcohol syndrome (fetal damage induced by alcohol).

Psychological manifestations

Apart from the psychological changes already described there are certain complicating syndromes, namely:

1 *Alcoholic hallucinosis.* A condition characterized by auditory hallucinations of long standing followed by the development of paranoid delusions. It is controversial whether this is a syndrome in its own right or merely the incidence of schizophrenia in an alcoholic.

Typically the onset is insidious and remits if the patient abstains from alcohol.

2 *Delirium tremens.* As the name implies this is a state of restlessness and impaired consciousness associated with tremor. The onset usually follows alcoholic withdrawal and may be heralded by a 24-hour prodromal period in which apprehension is prominent, also misinterpretation of the environment, mild disorientation and fits.

The florid clinical picture reveals an excited hallucinated (visually and aurally) patient, misinterpreting his environment in paranoid fashion and in an affective state of terror.

He is usually restless and febrile.

Treatment. Nursing in a darkened room, the provision of plenty of fluid, vitamin saturation and the use of phenothiazine tranquillizers will restore to normal contact with reality in under 36 hours. Chlormethiazole (Hemineverin) is also valuable, or Chlordiazepoxide 25 mg every 4 hours.

3 *Korsakov's syndrome.* A syndrome of gross impairment of recent memory with a tendency to confabulate answers. This syndrome was originally described in alcoholics but can also be caused by arteriosclerosis, etc.

4 *Alcoholic dementia.* There is nothing particular about the condition apart from the aetiology. An extremely insidious onset is the rule.

5 *Psycho-social complications.* (a) Marital breakdown; (b) loss of job; (c) general fall-off in personal relationships; (d) car accidents; (e) law breaking; or (f) aggressive behaviour and violence. All these lead to personal catastrophe and too often end in suicide.

Treatment and prevention

The first step in treatment is withdrawal from alcohol. This can only be achieved in hospital and the successful treatment of alcoholism depends on this initial step followed by abstention. Withdrawal is not difficult to manage; it requires a degree of cooperation which reflects the patient's intention to get rid of the habit. And of course, the patient is under no compulsion to do this.

There is no point in prolonging the agony by giving diminishing quantities of alcohol, it is better to stop completely and be prepared to treat any complications which follow, e.g. fits or delirium tremens. Sedatives such as barbiturates are best avoided in the withdrawal period; most workers prefer to use phenothiazine tranquillizers (Chlorpromazine, Promazine) to allay restlessness, combined with *vitamin saturation* and plenty of fluid and nourishment. Another valuable medication in alcohol withdrawal is Chlormethiazole (Hemineverin). This is a sedative and anticonvulsant that many regard as ideal. It can be given intravenously, e.g. in the case of associated severe illness. However, Hemineverin itself can cause dependence so that many prefer to use either Chlordiazepoxide 25 mg every 4 hours, or Diazepam 20 mg every 4 hours, in reducing doses over a 6-day period.

Once the withdrawal period is over one is faced with the problem of encouraging abstention from alcohol for the rest of the patient's life.

There are several ways of approaching this problem; none is complete in itself. First, by medication, disulfiram (antabuse) provides a chemical defence against alcohol for the patient so that if he takes a drink when on regular antabuse medication, he gets an unpleasant reaction in which he feels unwell, flushes and collapses. The success of this treatment depends on the degree of cooperation that the patient is willing to offer.

The main forms of help offered to the alcoholic are psychotherapeutic and social. Individual psychotherapy probably has little to offer the alcoholic, but the available evidence suggests that group psychotherapy in specialized units has, by helping the alcoholic to see his difficulties in perspective, and to come to terms with the problems that drink provides for him, and the problems created for him by abstention. Not least it may show him the problems that force him to drink. A telling comment on this was made by a patient who said, 'It's all very well asking me to give up drinking but what are you going to put in its place?'

Alcoholics Anonymous (A.A.) plays a great part in the treatment of the alcoholic and its help should be offered to all. It is an organization of alcoholics devoted to helping each other to abstain from drink and has the great merit of being founded on commonsense principles of a semi-religious sort. The symptomatic alcoholic is treated by treating the underlying condition, e.g. depression, etc.

Modification of drinking behaviour

It is now realized that for the majority of patients total abstention is impossible to achieve and, with this in mind, current practice favours re-educating the patient in learning to return to controlled, sensible drinking. This is of course not applicable to patients who have severe associated physical damage. Such patients have to work towards total abstention.

Prognosis

Prognosis is not precise but a few general comments can be made. The sounder the individual's personality the better the prognosis. The shorter the duration of alcoholism the better. Occupations leading to alcoholism make the prognosis worse (barmen, etc.).

Prevention

Could be aided by (a) increased taxation; (b) increased cost; (c) ban on advertising; and (d) educating people to drink moderately.

DRUG DEPENDENCE

Drug dependence continues to cause medical and social concern. This started in the U.K. in the early 1960s with the finding of an increased incidence of self-injection with opiates, heroin particularly, by young people. As might be expected careful examination of this phenomenon reveals that problems of drug misuse amongst the young were more extensive than had been realized. The whole problem should be viewed against a background of widespread consumption of psychotropic drugs in general by the population at large under medical supervision. The common drugs of dependence may be considered under three headings: stimulant, sedative and hallucinogenic drugs.

Drugs with a predominantly sedative-type action

These fall into two groups. First of all there are the sedative analgesics—in other words the opiate and opioid drugs of which the most highly prized by the user would be heroin and morphine. These are usually taken intravenously and a full blown syndrome of dependence is characterized by the presence of physical and psychological dependence, the former being manifest by physical withdrawal symptoms if the drug is discontinued and the latter by a good deal of personal involvement with drug use and often by the alteration in a person's way of life so that he becomes very closely involved with a life style in which drug usage is the main activity. This can end up with a state of social neglect where the user spends all his time and money getting hold of drugs and neglecting himself. There are no specific signs of dependence itself though injection marks on the arms and legs are common. The opiate abstinence syndrome includes restlessness, irritability, abdominal cramps, nausea, rhinitis and diarrhoea. Withdrawal from heroin should be carried out gradually and it is customary to use this period to improve the patient's physical state with vitamins, fluids, food and tranquillizers. Heroin is reduced gradually and replaced by methadone by mouth. This drug has the effect of a longer duration of action and is a valuable way of treating withdrawal symptoms. Detoxification is of course only the first stage and is followed by the most difficult aspects of treatment, namely, the encouragement of abstention. In general, encouraging patients towards abstention can be said to rest on two principles, the first of which is to try and find an alternative satisfaction in the patient's life to the use of drugs and this can be done by social means where one tries to provide the patient with a different life altogether. Notable examples of this sort of manoeuvre would be the Phoenix Houses, which started in America, where patients commit themselves to a drug-free life and work out their problems in vigorous open-encounter sessions. Though the relapse rate is high in opiate dependence it is unwise to take too pessimistic a view since a great deal can be done to improve the physical and psychological status of all drug users. The second approach is to try and substitute another drug for the heroin and current practice favours the use of Methadone in this respect.

Hypno-sedative drugs

These include barbiturates and a large number of non-barbiturate sedatives such as Methaqualone. The former are often prescribed in a rather unwise fashion, producing chronic barbiturate intoxication and dependence which may arise far more frequently than may be suspected. In chronic barbiturate intoxication are found slurred speech, nystagmus and ataxia with various states of confusion. Withdrawal from barbiturates often produces fits and the withdrawal period should be treated by gradual detoxification, using pentobarbitone in divided doses reducing by 100 mg daily. It should be noted that benzodiazepenes, in particular Diazepam, can produce states of chronic dependency when taken in doses in excess of the normal therapeutic level and that withdrawal symptoms including withdrawal seizures may occur.

Stimulant drugs

The commonest in use are those of the amphetamine type including dexedrine, drinamyl, amphetamine and preludin. These drugs, taken by people of normal and abnormal personality for their stimulant effect produce a short-lived feeling of well-being followed by gloom inducing the taker to consume larger quantities of the drug so that up to 2 g per 24 hours may be consumed.

States of *restlessness and irritability* with outbursts of anger are common but probably the most serious manifestation is *amphetamine psychosis* (Connell 1954). This is a syndrome of restlessness, elation, paranoid ideas and hallucinosis, i.e. a schizophreniform psychosis which clears up on withdrawal.

The treatment of amphetamine dependence is made more difficult by its prevalence amongst psychopaths and also by its unwise prescription. It should be emphasized that the clear indications for the uses of amphetamines are really only three: narcolepsy, in oversedated epileptic patients, and in the treatment of hyperkinetic children.

In recent years, cocaine has become a widely used stimulant taken by inhalation.

Hallucinogenic drugs

Hallucinogenic drugs have been more widely misused in recent years since the early 1960s. The most commonly misused drug is lysergic acid (LSD) and although it does not produce any physical dependence it certainly can cause states of psychological dependence where the individual overvalues its supposed effects on his mental state. Unhappily LSD is associated with adverse reactions and in general these tend to fall into three types: states of acute psychotic excitement, chronic depressive states, and states of panic and terror, often followed by persistent symptoms of depersonalization. Fortunately the majority of LSD-adverse reactions appear to subside relatively spontaneously though ideally such patients should receive psychiatric supervision and admission where necessary.

Other hallucinogenic drugs which may be encountered include Phencyclidine (PCP) which is becoming a fairly widely used 'street' drug.

Aetiology

Better understanding of the pharmacology of drug dependence has been achieved by the identification of drug receptors, in particular, opiate receptors in the brain and central nervous system. In addition, the identification of naturally occurring pentapeptides in the brain—the encephalins—which have opiate-like properties leading to the hypothesis that chronic opiate abuse would suppress the activity of encephalins thus accounting for the onset of withdrawal symptoms when the drug is discontinued.

People rarely become dependent on drugs by accident, for example severe therapeutic dependence remains uncommon. It should be remembered that dependency-producing drugs are in general 'mind altering', i.e. they may affect feeling, perception, thinking and behaviour. Also the user will have heard about the supposed effects and wants to try them out. This means that dependence may follow a repeated, pleasant, drug-induced effect or follow the use of a drug which abolishes some unpleasant subjective symptoms and these include not only the abolition of withdrawal symptoms, but in some cases neurotic anxiety etc., so that the drug becomes a form of self-medication.

The terms 'hard' and 'soft' drugs are misleading. A more useful distinction may however be drawn between those who inject themselves with drugs and those who swallow them. The former group are more likely to develop severe varieties of dependence and fairly quickly at that, also they have an associated morbidity and mortality from the effects of unsterile self-injection.

Society is presently most concerned about drug use amongst young males for hedonic reasons. But these patients, though they present urgent social problems should not deflect interest in the wider problems of 'hidden' dependency on sedatives, hypnotics and tranquillizers.

A useful way of regarding drug dependence is to realize that it often involves 'drug-using behaviour', i.e. a life style, rather than mere pharmacological dependence. At present youthful drug dependence is

Chapter 6

notable for subcultural drug use, and attitudes and a view of the world that may go with it. Multiple drug use is becoming more common.

Drug dependence, though it may ostensibly be related to such ephemera as 'curiosity', 'a new experience' etc. is in severe cases an outgrowth of longstanding personality disorder—often of psychopathic dimensions, but this *does not account for all cases.* Some may use drugs to relieve anxiety and depression or as a barrier between themselves and a world which they find unacceptable. While for the delinquency-oriented youngster drugs may provide an easy source of illicit gratification.

Regarding the aetiology of drug dependence, facts are hard to come by. Speculation is universal.

Drugs come and go. Ten years ago cocaine use had virtually disappeared. At present in the U.S.A. it has reached epidemic proportions. The same may be said of the spread of inhalation of volatile solvents in certain parts of the U.K.

REFERENCES

Bewley T. H. (1965) Heroin addiction in the U.K. (1954–1964). *Br. med. J.*, ii, 1284.

Bewley T. H. (1965) Heroin and cocaine addiction. *Lancet*, i, 808.

Connell P. H. (1958) *Amphetamine Psychosis.* Chapman & Hall, London.

Edwards G. & Gross M. M. (1976) Alcohol dependence: provisional description of a clinical syndrome. *Br. med. J.*, i, 1058.

Jellinek E. M. (1960) Alcoholism, a genus and some of its species. *Canad. med. Ass. J.*, 83, 1341.

Kessel N. & Grossman G. (1961) Suicide in alcoholics. *Br. med. J.*, ii, 1671.

National Council on Alcoholism (1972) Criteria for the diagnosis of alcoholism. *Am. J. Psychiatry*, 119, 127.

Szasz T. (1975) *Ceremonial chemistry—The Ritual Persecution of Drug Addicts and Pushers.* Routledge and Kegan Paul, London.

W.H.O. Expert Committee on Mental Health (1955) Alcohol and Alcoholism. *Tech Rep. W.H.O.* No. 94.

Willis J. H. (1969) *Drug Dependence.* Faber, London.

CHAPTER 7
PSYCHOSEXUAL DISORDERS

Introduction

It is only in the last few years that any reference to psychosexual disorders has had any place in the undergraduate medical curriculum. This was really an amazing gap in the training of doctors since it left them with very limited understanding of common sexual problems and meant that they were unable to offer any advice or help at all in many cases. This was probably backed up by a hangover from more prudish attitudes of the past when the discussion of sexual matters at any level was practically taboo. There were of course a number of physicians and psychiatrists who had interest and ability to deal with the problems of patients with psychosexual disorders but they were relatively few and the literature was sparse. Above and beyond this there was little experimental work to back up many of the pronouncements on psychosexual topics which were made mainly on the basis of untested theories, often highly speculative. However, in more recent times, starting with the work of Kinsey on the varieties of sexual practice in the American population and more recently with the experimental work of Masters and Johnston on the treatment of common psychosexual disorders, the topic has at last found its place in undergraduate medical teaching. We may add to this the fact that public demand for help with their sexual problems naturally became greater as the public became aware through the media that research and active therapy was available in various parts of the world, notably the U.S.A.

Patients with sexual problems undergo a great deal of unhappiness and misery and if help is not available it can lead to marital breakdown, depressive states, alcohol abuse, drug abuse and suicidal attempts. Clearly the management of psychosexual disorders is not entirely the province of the physician, in fact contemporary approaches to these problems involves a multidisciplinary approach in which physicians, psychiatrist, psychologists and social workers will all make their relevant contributions. But the doctor is frequently the first person consulted and there are recognizable groups of common psychosexual problems that every doctor should know about. The most common psychosexual problems include:

1   erectile failure, i.e. impotence in the male;
2   premature ejaculation; and
3   failure to achieve orgasm in the female. This term is preferable to frigidity which is really an unhappy term which should be dropped.

ERECTILE FAILURE

Erectile failure is simply related to anxiety based on fear of loss of sexual potency and this can arise in various ways; probably the commonest are ignorance, inexperience or long standing fears about potency which may go well back into puberty. Another common cause is that of the person who fails to achieve erection at the first attempt at sexual intercourse. This sort of erectile failure may convince the man that he is incapable of achieving erection and repeated failures reinforce the condition, leaving the patient with the belief that the disorder is quite untreatable. Approximately 90% of cases of erectile failure arise out of anxiety, but there are obviously important physical causes including neurological disorders such as diabetic neuropathy and spinal cord lesions and also it may be found in patients whose general physical health is below par, e.g. through chronic cardiac disorders. Endocrine causes of erectile failure are actually relatively rare but obviously need to be borne in mind. At the present time it should be remembered that there are many drugs that patients may be taking that will contribute to erectile failure. Any hypno-sedative or tranquillizer taken regularly will lead to this; perhaps the commonest of these is alcohol in excess and certainly all the tricyclic antidepressants produce this as a side-effect. It is also found in patients who are taking antihypertensive medications.

Treatment

A full and detailed history of the patient's sexual development, range of experience and attitudes towards sexuality is a prerequisite. Having excluded physical or pharmacological causes, one is left in the vast majority of cases with a patient whose failure is related to anxiety. The impotent patient cannot be treated on his own. It is important always to secure the cooperation of the sexual partner and go very carefully into all the details of the development of the patient's impotence. Having established the extent of the problem, the usual recommendation is to advise partners to abstain from sexual intercourse. The value of this is that it helps both the patient and the partner to have a cooling-off period where the resentment, ill-feeling and general wretchedness that have usually built up can be allowed to subside. It is also important to make it clear to both that this is a treatable condition, with the doctor positive, supportive and encouraging in attitude. Space does not permit a detailed examination of the various therapeutic techniques involved but the principles can be summarized by saying that the first essential is to clarify the history from the point of view of both partners as fully as possible, to advise a period of abstention for several weeks and then to commence upon therapy. The general principles of therapy now employed tend to involve the patient in a process of re-education so that sexual activity is approached without anxiety and the partner is advised not to react in a rejecting and unhappy way if erection is not achieved but gradually to build up sexual activity without aiming at complete penetration. The idea then is to rehabilitate the lost sexual function in a non-stressful way, thus by gaining confidence, the patient's erections will return to normal and satisfactory sexual intercourse will then follow. Prognosis is notoriously difficult but there does seem now to be a consensus of opinion that if a man has been impotent for a period in excess of 2 years then success rates are extremely low, below 2 years success rates may be as high as 80% or more.

PREMATURE EJACULATION

Premature ejaculation is extremely common, and again causes great unhappiness and bitterness on the part of the disappointed sexual partner; but it is probably the most treatable of psychosexual disorders, provided the full cooperation of the partner is available. Contemporary mainstay of therapy is to advise the partner to compress the glans penis firmly just before ejaculation and this will inhibit it. If this is followed by a period of rest, intercourse may be recommenced and ejaculation delayed. It is merely a question of practice.

FAILURE OF FEMALE ORGASM

This is probably one of the unhappiest areas of psychosexual dysfunction. For many years it was claimed that the female orgasm was caused by vaginal stimulation by the erect penis and many women found themselves labelled as frigid because this did not seem to occur. In fact, they felt cheated, disappointed and often felt themselves less than fully female because they had not achieved this widely described experience. However, experimental evidence has shown that in fact female orgasm is mainly caused by clitoral stimulation and that the vaginal orgasm is relatively rare, again, with good cooperation between sexual partners and advice about clitoral stimulation, manual, oral and for that matter mechanical, most women who may have been labelled 'frigid' for years are able to achieve satisfactory orgasm and happy sexual relations which they felt had previously been denied to them.

SEXUAL DEVIATIONS

Here we face problems of definition, in the past male and female homosexuality were considered to be sexual deviations but the present view is that this is not the case and that male and female homosexuals are normal variants, so that attempts to change a person's sexual orientation from homosexual to heterosexual is now rarely attempted except in those cases where the patient particularly requests it. At the same time it has to be remembered that homosexuals of either sex are often the victims of a good deal of persecution by society that regards their sexual lives as immoral and disgusting and this can lead to a great deal of unhappiness particularly in young male homosexuals who can become severely depressed and make suicidal attempts. Homosexuals therefore are perhaps more vulnerable to mood disturbance, guilty feelings, etc. than otherwise, and will need sympathetic and straightforward counselling in order to help them to live with themselves. Public attitudes have softened to a certain extent, and for that matter, homosexual acts between male consenting adults are no longer against the law, but this has not removed from the homosexual a considerable amount of unhappiness and vulnerability. Another point that is important is to recognize that we distinguish between homosexual orientation that is a person whose sexual preference is entirely for the same sex, and homosexual behaviour. By homosexual behaviour we refer to homosexual acts which occur in highly specialized situations, in other words in one-sex communities where no heterosexual outlet is available. Another point that needs sympathetic care encompasses the problem that many young adolescents may have regarding their sexual identity: they may have doubts as to whether or not they are homosexual or heterosexual. Sensible psychotherapy will usually help them to solve this problem.

Fetishism

This is usually regarded as a sexual deviation and implies that condition where the person may only achieve orgasm after being stimulated by various inanimate objects ranging from shoes, black rubber raincoats to even more bizarre outfits.

Sadism and masochism

These are on the whole to be regarded as serious and often dangerous sexual deviations since they include enjoyment of pain or of the infliction of pain as a sexual preamble before orgasm and it will be wise always to refer such patients who ask for help to a psychiatrist.

Transvestism
(often called cross-dressing)

Transvestism merely means the drive, in the male usually, to dress up in female clothing, either as a way of obtaining sexual relief or before having heterosexual intercourse. It has some relation to homosexuality. It would be difficult to say whether this is a state that needs treating: probably the most important criterion is if the transvestite is made unhappy by it or if his sexual partner is.

Trans-sexualism

This means the desire to change sex. This is an entirely different area from transvestism and is mainly seen in men who wish to become female. They are often extremely determined in this way and will undergo extensive surgery, penile amputation and the creation of an artificial vagina, breast implants and so on. Psychiatry has not been successful in persuading trans-sexualists to change their attitudes to this. The really determined trans-sexualist will attain his goal if at all possible.

No one really knows what is the outcome of a man who has a surgically created artificial vagina and breast implants and becomes outwardly female in appearance, and limited experience suggests that too often trans-sexualism overlies quite deep-seated personality problems even to the extent of serious personality disorder. The ethics of sex transformation are in this author's opinion highly questionable.

REFERENCES

Kinsey A. C., Pomeroy W. B. & Martin C. E. (1948) *Sexual Behavior in the Human Male.* Saunders, Philadelphia.

Kinsey A. C., Pomeroy W. B., Martin C. E. & Gebhard (1953) *Sexual Behavior in the Human Female.* Saunders, Philadelphia.

Masters W. H. & Johnson V. E. (1970) *Human Sexual Inadequacy.* Little Brown, Boston.

CHAPTER 8
MENTAL SUBNORMALITY
(MENTAL IMPAIRMENT)

Introduction

People who are found to have 'arrested or incomplete' mental development from birth are usually described as being mentally subnormal. Their fundamental defect is one of intelligence. However, they usually have other degrees of psychological and social handicap which may be accompanied by physical disabilities, often severe. It is important to be aware of the many problems and difficulties that may beset the subnormal patient. Failure to recognize this from the start can result in the subnormal missing out on the detailed attention, advice and treatment which he and his relatives need. This awareness of the complexity of the problems of subnormality has led to a more hopeful attitude in management and treatment.

INTELLIGENCE

Intelligence is a hypothetical concept which is taken to encompass individual differences that exist in a presumed innate set of attributes that are the expression of a general ability which enables the individual to learn from experience, form judgements, handle concepts and modify behaviour. Intelligence is not regarded as a fixed unvarying entity but as something which is modifiable by environment, i.e. by education and favourable upbringing. Also it appears that the extent to which people utilize their intelligence is influenced by their levels of motivation, emotional stability and maturity. Much experimental evidence suggests that intelligence is multifactorial, that is to say, a general level of ability subsumes certain special abilities all of which correlate highly with each other.

Measurement of intelligence

A person's level of intelligence is commonly related to the intelligence quotient (IQ), a numerical method which is usually a measurable, valid and reliable way of representing intelligence levels. Originally it was estimated with reference to 'mental' age and chronological age since the earliest attempts to measure intelligence took the mental age as the unit of measurement, but IQ measurement has moved away from this and, at the present time, the measurement of intelligence is based on estimations of the deviations from the mean scores obtained by individuals in the same groups as the person being tested. Tests are standardized by being given to a representative sample of a population, stratified by age. For any given age group, the mean score obtained is given an arbitrary value of 100, i.e. the average IQ is assumed to be 100, and the standard deviation of IQ levels is set at 15 points.

In this way, when the distribution of IQ's is plotted it is found that, like the distribution of stature, the curve approximates to the so called 'normal' distribution. That is to say the majority of cases cluster around the mean, and cases which differ markedly from the mean are comparatively rare.

Using a standardized intelligence test, approximately one-half of the population will score between 90 and 110 points and about two-thirds between 85 and 115 points. Of the population 95% will have IQ's between 70 and 130, i.e. two standard deviations either side of the mean.

On the whole, lower intelligence is rather more common than high intelligence or put in statistical terms the curve is negatively skewed. This suggests that while the majority of individuals of low intelligence are normal variants, there are a certain proportion whose intellectual defect arises as a result of disease, injury or metabolic disturbance.

However, it has to be recognized that since the IQ is to a large extent an arbitrary score, it is difficult to be precise about the true distribution of intelligence. With this in mind, it can be seen that the intelligence quotient, particularly when the figure is low, can be very misleading without a total appreciation of the psychological and social characteristics of the person being examined. The estimation of subnormality of intelligence is therefore made by measuring the IQ. At present, the cut off points are that subnormality of intelligence is said to exist if the IQ is below 70 points and severe subnormality if the IQ is below 50 points.

However, the position is made somewhat more difficult by the Mental Health Act which defines both subnormality and severe subnormality without reference to psychometry.

In the Mental Health Act the subnormal are defined as persons suffering from a 'state of arrested or incomplete development of mind (not amounting to severe subnormality) which includes subnormality of intelligence and is of a nature or degree which requires or is susceptible to medical or other special care or training of the patient'. This attempt at categorization would include those patients formerly described as 'feeble minded'.

Though severe subnormality is officially diagnosed if the IQ is below 50, this applies only to a small proportion of the population. Children who are handicapped to this extent are unlikely ever to be able to work except in a highly sheltered environment. Of the total population around 3% are found to have IQ's below 70, and about 3 per 1000 to have an IQ below 50. This means that the numbers of the severely mentally handicapped are small, but the modestly handicapped, i.e. 70 to 90 IQ are considerably greater and represent an important group for whom a good deal more can be done in terms of education and training than is generally realized. In the case of these mildly handicapped patients social factors are often as important as genetic or organic factors in causation (Birch *et al.* 1970) as opposed to the severely subnormal, most of whom have organic brain damage. The severely subnormal are more prone to psychosis, fits and behaviour disturbance in general (Rutter *et al.* 1971). However, the mildly subnormal present an entirely different set of social, clinical and educational problems.

Many subnormal patients are otherwise 'normal' people whose intelligence is in the extreme low ranges of the frequency distribution curve. Others, however, are individuals of potentially higher intelligence who have experienced brain damage. The latter would include those affected by rubella in the first 3 months of fetal life or head injury or encephalitis in infancy. Others include individuals with genetically determined metabolic disorders which inhibit normal brain development and function.

On the other hand there are individuals who are subnormal by reason of intellectual, emotional or social deprivation in early life. A child reared in a brutalizing atmosphere is likely to score many points lower on IQ tests than another child of equal ability coming from a more favourable home. It should be remembered too that limited intelligence does not mean that the patient lacks commonsense. Clinical experience of interviewing the subnormal patient constantly reaffirms this fact.

In addition to all this subnormal patients may be handicapped by poor vision or deafness which prevent them from making the most effective use of their available intelligence. Disturbances such as epilepsy or birth-induced cerebral palsy are common and provide further handicap. Subnormal patients are often, but not always, emotionally as well as intellectually immature. Also the severely subnormal often has a dysplastic physique with a small brain and head and may display hyperkinetic syndromes in childhood.

Aetiology of mental subnormality

Some idea of the growth of clearer understanding of the range of causes of mental subnormality may be gathered from the fact that while in 1954 a standard textbook of psychiatry listed eight syndromes of known aetiology, by 1968 another standard text was able to list over forty-five. This is a reflection of the impetus to research into mental subnormality that has followed the influence of the realization that the mentally subnormal had been neglected and the specific influence of key discoveries such as that of Lejeune (1959) who showed that Down's syndrome (mongolism) was associated with forty-seven chromosomes, instead of the normal forty-six. This stimulated interest in cytogenetic research. Interest in inborn metabolic errors was stimulated by the discovery of phenylketonuria (PKU). Mental subnormality caused by inherited metabolic disorders is said to comprise less than 4% of the total population of the mentally subnormal, but this is in the light of presently available information. Better understanding of cytogenetics and cerebral enzyme systems may reveal further inherited disorders as yet unsuspected. The first metabolic disorder to be discovered as a cause of subnormality was phenylketonuria.

Phenylketonuria (phenylpyruvic oligophrenia) (PKU) is a disorder transmitted by autosomal recessive inheritance and is caused by a deficiency of the enzyme phenylalanine hydroxylase which normally converts phenylalanine to tyrosine. This deficiency leads not only to a raised blood phenylalanine and a corresponding urinary excretion of phenylpyruvic acid but also defective cerebral biochemistry usually resulting in severe mental handicap. The majority of patients have EEG abnormalities and around 30% have fits. Motor and coordinative symptoms are common, as are restricted growth and speech disorders. Treatment is based on screening using urinary testing to detect phenylpyruvic acid. The treatment consists of a diet free of phenylalanine. The best results are achieved if the condition is detected within 6 months of birth. Phenylketonuria causes a deficiency of tryptophan which is a precursor of 5-HT (serotonin), a known central transmitting substance, possibly implicated in severe depression such as is caused by reserpine.

Disturbances of protein metabolism causing subnormality include phenylketonuria, and other rare conditions all characterized by aminoaciduria. They include Hartnup disease, transmitted by autosomal recessive inheritance. Often symptoms vary and may represent in adolescence with personality change since symptoms can be mild. The basic manifestations include a pellagrinous rash, cerebellar symptoms and subnormality. The metabolic deficit involves tryptophan metabolism. Maple sugar disease is caused by defective metabolism of leucine, isoleucine and valine, all of which are excreted in the urine, producing a characteristic odour. Autosomal recessive inheritance is the mode of transmission and symptoms come on early with fits and organic deterioration. Dietary treatment, i.e. restricting the amino acids involved, is used and the results are said to be promising.

Other, much rarer inherited metabolic defects involving protein metabolism include histidinaemia, citrullinuria, argininosuccinic aciduria, hyperglycinaemia, homocystinuria and others. Their importance lies in their recognition by chromatographic screening of urine and blood and in the fact that recognition of one such rarity may lead to another and suggest further lines of research.

Carbohydrate disturbances include galactosaemia, transmitted by autosomal recessive inheritance. The basic deficiency is the absence of the enzyme Galactose 1 phosphate uridyltransferase. The onset comes on with milk feeding and may be fatal or lead to severe subnormality, hepatic failure and fits. Dietary treatment started early, prevents the disorder developing, hence the importance of early recognition. Von Gierke's disease, a glycogen storage disease, transmitted by autosomal recessive inheritance, is characterized by generalized glycogen deposits, hepatomegaly, fits and subnormality. Other inherited disorders of carbohydrate metabolism include hypoglycaemia, fructose intolerance and sucrosuria.

Disorders of lipoid metabolism include cerebromacular degenerations—Tay Sach's disease, this is transmitted by autosomal recessive inheritance. The onset is early with weakness, failure to thrive, spasticity and macular degeneration (cherry red spot). The basic defect consists in the accumulation of lipids (gangliosides) in neurones. There are a number of clinical types, the disorder is chiefly found in Eastern European Jews. Niemann Pick's disease, again autosomal recessive inheritance, is found mainly in Jews and consists in sphingomyelin storage caused by enzyme deficiency, Gaucher's disease is caused by failure of the enzyme that acts on glucocerebroside.

Progressive leucoencephalopathies include Schilder's disease and Merzbacher Pelizaeus disease. Other metabolic causes include cretinism, hypoparathyroidism, idiopathic hypercalcaemia, Hurler's disease, caused by the accumulation of mucopolysaccharides, and Wilson's disease. It should be emphasized that these are all rare and depend for recognition on awareness of family history and proper screening.

Chromosomal abnormalities leading to subnormality

Down's syndrome

In 1887 Langdon–Down described a syndrome of mental handicap associated with various physical abnormalities and a supposed resemblance to members of the Mongol race. This was a mistake and gave rise to discontent with the use of the term. The preferred name is now Down's syndrome. The incidence is approximately 1 in 600 births which makes it a relatively common type of mental handicap, the majority of those affected being severely subnormal. Patients tend to have a characteristic appearance with a 'typical' face—brachycephaly, short neck, epicanthic folds on the medial aspect of the eyes, short fingers, transverse tongue fissures, congenital heart lesions. In fact over 100 associated physical abnormalities have now been described.

In 1959 Lejeune, Gauthier and Turpin demonstrated the presence of an extra chromosome in Down's syndrome (forty-seven instead of forty-six). The extra chromosome provided 3 at 21 instead of 2, hence the name Trisomy 21. This opened up a whole new field of research into cytogenetics and mental subnormality.

It is now generally agreed that there are at least three variants of Down's syndrome. The first is Trisomy 21 as originally described by Lejeune *et al.*

This is the commonest variety of the syndrome and is accounted for by non-disjunction of unknown aetiology. The second variety is caused by translocation, with fusion of chromosomes 15 and 21. This is an inherited disorder, an important point when prognosis is under discussion. The third type 'partial Down's syndrome' is probably caused by chromosomal mosaicism, i.e. a mixture of trisomy and normal autosomes.

Other autosomal trisomic conditions and defects are also described these include:

1   *Trisomy 13/15 (Patau's syndrome).* There is severe subnormality,

limited survival, scalp defects, polydactyly, narrow temples, septal defects, hypertelorism and epilepsy.

2 *Trisomy 17/18 (Edward's syndrome).* There is severe subnormality, micrognathia, hypertelorism, flexion of fingers, diaphragmatic hernia, kidney abnormalities.

3 *Cri du chat.* This syndrome is caused by partial deletion of 5 chromosome. Severe subnormality is associated with many congenital defects and a characteristic cry likened to a kitten or a seagull.

Other cytogenetic abnormalities associated with mental handicap include sex linked disorders such as:

1 *Klinefelter's syndrome.* The genetic constitution is XXY although XXXY, and mosaics of XX and XXY have been described. The usual clinical picture is of testicular atrophy, girlish voice, tall angular build and gynaecomastia, usually recognized at adolescence. The syndrome is perfectly compatible with normal intelligence but subnormality can and does occur. Psychiatric problems are, not surprisingly, common in this syndrome.

2 *Turner's syndrome.* Here the genetic sex constitution is XO and the syndrome includes dwarfism, webbing of the neck, ovarian agenesis and cubitus valgus. Mental subnormality is usually mild, normal intelligence is more common however.

3 *The XYY syndrome.* This is associated with tall stature, mild subnormality and delinquent behaviour.

Other known types of mental subnormality associated with genetic inheritance include microcephaly, tuberose sclerosis, a triad of epilepsy, adenoma sebaccum and subnormality associated with renal and cardiac tumours. There are rarities also such as the Sturge–Weber syndromes with haemangiomata of face, retinal vascular abnormalities and cerebral calcification and the Lawrence–Moon–Biedl syndrome where there is pituitary dysfunction, polydactyly, retinitis pigmentosa and subnormality.

At the end of this list of known genetic causes we are left with the fact that once external causes such as maternal infection, especially rubella, syphilis, anoxia, malnutrition and trauma, have been excluded, the mass of the mentally retarded are normal variants, and that the recognition of handicap may occur at a wide range on the child's time scale.

For example the newborn may give rise to suspected subnormality because of small size, failure to thrive and fits. In practice, unless the baby has associated gross abnormalities, subnormality is unlikely to be detected in the first year of life. Poor progress in childhood is something that may raise suspicion, there again if the child has a biochemically identifiable lesion then the diagnosis is confirmed; otherwise it will depend on overall assessment of its abilities in all directions and will be largely determined as a case for investigation by the expectations of the family concerned. Failure of the development of speech is probably one of the commonest presenting complaints. Poor school progress comes later as a symptom to be evaluated. Kirman (1958) listed the times of appearance of the first symptom in 233 mentally handicapped children from birth to 48 months. They included physical features (sixty-one), eye defect (twenty-nine), slow (forty-three), not sitting (thirty-four), not walking (sixteen) as opposed to much less common things, e.g. cerebral palsy (six), not crawling (twenty), destructive (one). In the first 5 years of life the child needs the fullest possible assessment by doctor, psychologist and social worker in order to establish the extent of the handicap.

The family of the subnormal patient

The handicaps of the mentally subnormal, as have been mentioned, do not end with intellectual deficit. Many authors, especially Rutter (1972) and Rutter *et al.* (1970) have pointed out that in the subnormal there is a higher incidence of neurosis, personality disorder, antisocial behaviour and developmental disorders. Also rare disorders, such as hyperkinesis and infantile psychosis, are more common in retarded children but they are not typical, i.e. peculiar to retarded children in whom there can occur a heterogeneous distribution of psychiatric disturbance and behaviour problems. Rutter (1972) also emphasizes that deviant behaviour is more common in children of average intelligence than in those of superior intelligence and more frequent in those of lower IQ than in those of average IQ.

Rutter relates the psychological disadvantages more to brain malfunction than to lost function and emphasizes the importance of the adverse influences of social rejection, institutional treatment and adverse effects of medication. If we add to this the limited educational attainments and problems of the retarded child the spectrum of potential and real psychological disadvantage becomes complete. The management of the problems of subnormality is then a complex procedure which must always take into account not only the identification of special syndromes and the management of associated physical handicap but also the emotional, social and cultural disadvantages that may hinder his attaining the best possible level of achievement.

Management of the subnormal patient

Children

Subnormal children develop better both from the point of view of intelligence and social ability if they spend their childhood with the family. Parents can accept the subnormal child as long as they are given sensible explanation and advice. It is vital to recognize that the parents may feel incompetent, helpless, resentful, frustrated, i.e. experience a wide variety of conflicting emotions when confronted with the realization that the child is handicapped in this way. It is therefore particularly important that advice and support should be readily available when the abnormality is first recognized or when slow development is first suspected by either parent, doctor or health visitor. Full paediatric assessment is essential so that treatable metabolic disorders may be discovered. In addition sensory handicaps such as blindness or deafness should be recognized. The problems of speech disorder, dyslexia and epilepsy may be recognized.

Educational requirements

The majority of children with IQ's over 55 are 'educable' in that they will be able to learn the rudiments of reading and writing and attend schools run by their Education Authority. Those who are most backward in this group are classified as educationally subnormal and sent to special schools.

Children with IQ's below 50 are excluded from school though the majority can benefit from education given in day training centres, run by the local authority. The majority of ESN school leavers manage to function as ordinary if somewhat limited people when they leave school and only a minority ever come to the notice of the local Mental Health Authority. Most of them settle down in time, find work, and present no great problem. A few may require institutional care which in every case should be on a voluntary basis to either residential home or hospital.

Severely subnormal children often make extremely good progress at day training centres and many achieve adult life able to work in sheltered surroundings. The most severely handicapped, and it must be emphasized that these are a minority, require to be fed and dressed and have long term care. After childhood, long stay hospital care will be necessary.

There are two definite indications for long term care of the subnormal or the severely subnormal individual away from home. They are:

1   Possibility of obtaining better education or treatment of a degree sufficient to outweigh the disadvantages of being away from home.

2   Where the patient's family is suffering from his presence in the home.

Thus it emerges that the criteria for admission to long stay hospitals for the mentally subnormal are largely social.

While it is true that a proportion of severely subnormal patients may require prolonged hospital care, it is increasingly realized that the basic needs of these patients are the same as those of their more generously endowed fellows, i.e. they need affection, warmth, social acceptance, education and employment. Given the right sort of environment any subnormal patient can find a more congenial and productive life in the community than he can in an institution. With this in mind, day centres, occupational training centres and the like, are excellent examples of the sort of community-orientated projects that foster enlightened care of such patients.

Subnormal patients can and do learn tasks that were previously supposed to be beyond their level of ability, providing that the teaching is carried out in a sensible patient way.

Tasks may need to be broken down in various ways and the patient may need to learn via one sensory channel rather than by being given a variety of instructions all at the same time. Above all he needs a climate where failure is not penalized and where emotional outbursts are accepted with sympathy and understanding.

The family of the subnormal child need help if they are to keep him at home or if he has to go into hospital. This help includes not only practical advice but also psychological support and understanding of the emotional problems posed by his very being. Guilt, resentment, anxiety, overprotection and denial are all common reactions and merit sensible acceptance and free discussion between doctor and parents. This is one area where such communication can be of inestimable value.

In considering the various possible causes of subnormality it cannot be too strongly emphasized that the majority of cases are normal variants who form between 2.5 and 3% of all children and that the majority of such handicapped children have mild defects (Rutter 1972) and that in their problems the aetiology is as much social as biological (Birch *et al.* 1970).

REFERENCES

Rutter M., Birch H. C., Thomas A. & Chess S. (1964) Temperamental characteristics in infancy and the later development of behavioural disorders. *Br. J. Psychiatry*, **110**, 651.

Rutter M., Graham P. & Yule W. (1970a) *A Neuropsychiatric Study in Childhood.* Spastics International Medical Publications and Heinemann, London.

Rutter M., Tizard J. & Whitmore K. (1970b) *Education, Health and Behaviour.* Longmans, London.

CHAPTER 9
DISORDERS OF CHILDHOOD
AND ADOLESCENCE

Introduction

Child psychiatry and child guidance are two terms that need clarifying. Child psychiatry is concerned with the recognition, diagnosis and treatment of the psychiatric syndromes of childhood. Child guidance is less clearly defined. It is concerned more with the recognition of neurotic and behaviour disorders, the counselling of delinquent and maladjusted children and is a good example of the use of a multidisciplinary team since the first Child Guidance Clinics were staffed by teams of psychologists, social workers and psychiatrists. Over the years, the rather artificial division between child psychiatry and child guidance has disappeared. The investigation of psychological and allied disorders in childhood and adolescence is based on a comprehensive assessment of the child and its family, taking into consideration not only emotional and intellectual difficulties that the child may have but also the overall development of the child, physical, neurological and psychological, in as comprehensive a fashion as possible.

The emotional difficulties of childhood and the problems of children in relationships with parents and peers, which may lead to symptoms and syndromes, have never been easy to classify. This is probably because children are, after all, developing and maturing individuals with a great capacity for change and this may have led to a tendency to suppose that, perhaps, classification might not be necessary. In the past, psychiatric disorders in childhood may have been universally described in terms of their relationship to apparent specific dynamic mechanisms. This view is probably too simplistic. Its validity has been challenged by long-term studies such as those of Rutter *et al.* (1971). Such surveys of the physical and emotional development of children have indicated that the 'disturbed child' has a high expectation of associated parental physical ill-health and that 'disturbed' children have a higher than average loading with poor physical health, minor neurological deficits and epilepsy. Another important problem regarding classification is that children's symptoms do not cluster into the syndromes of adult psychiatric disturbance in a convenient way. Also, the emotional problems and difficulties that they have vary with the passage of time. Above all, their personalities are not set in the rigid patterns of adult life. There is still disagreement about what may constitute the abnormal. Bed-wetting is of no significance in a child of 3 or 4 years, but is of considerable significance in a adolescent of 17.

However, some classification is needed. An easy method is to list those disorders which are more or less age-related, recognizing that there is considerable overlap.

CHILDHOOD

In childhood up to the age of 12 years, the most common disturbances, apart from epilepsy, specific learning defects and mental retardation, are disorders involving eating and excretion.

Eating disorders

Food refusal

Children like food. The baby is happy at the breast where he receives excellent nourishment, close bodily contact and obvious stimuli associated with maternal care. In other words, an enjoyable experience which is positively reinforced every time it is repeated. Baby feeding is, therefore, a rational practice in which the object is to nourish the baby in a loving way. Nevertheless, in the weaning period, when the baby stops sucking, he has to learn to feed in a way that is emotionally more neutral. Here, feeding problems can occur. These are usually straightforward and the majority of babies learn how to eat. Food refusal, characterized by flat refusal to eat, holding the food in the mouth or vomiting, can be extremely worrying and even alarming. Even quite small infants apparently sense the anxiety that this can create thus leading to a sort of power struggle between mother and child that can be prolonged well into childhood. Simple positive reassurance here is extremely valuable.

Obesity

Obesity leads to a high morbidity and mortality in adult life. Many fat children are encouraged to overeat by misguided, well-meaning parents or they may have been brought up in fat families where everyone eats too much. Some children overeat when they are unhappy and create for themselves a vicious circle where they eat more when mocked by others and then end up even fatter and more unhappy. This can persist through adolescence into adult life.

Disorders of excretion and elimination

These are seen at a later age in childhood where the reflex series of bowel/bladder evacuation are transferred from the casual demands of emptying into the napkin to precisely defined and socially determined situations, i.e. the pot and then the W.C. This arbitrary change in behaviour is not all that precise. Adults, even sober adults, sometimes urinate and defaecate in lay-bys, gardens or the street. Regular, unseen elimination is reinforced by building technology—it should be remembered that the Palace of Versailles was befouled by the faeces of visitors, especially ladies who wore so much clothing that all they could do was evacuate on the stairs. However, modern sanitation makes this unnecessary and undesirable. This is in sharp contrast to a society whose streets are fouled with animal excreta that contribute significantly to public health problems to an extent that has been only lately recognized.

In the child, the two obvious elimination problems are enuresis (bed-wetting) and encopresis (faecal soiling).

Enuresis

Toilet training consists essentially of teaching the infant to learn to associate the stimulus sequence of pot/bottom with parental pleasure and a clean nappy. In learning bladder control the infant is faced with a harder task since the bladder stimuli are often harder to perceive in sleep. One thing is certain and that is that fear and anxiety do cause unexpected bed-wetting, e.g. a 10-year-old boy, normally dry, was admitted to hospital after an accident. He wet the bed regularly in hospital and stopped as soon as he came home. This is a simple example as opposed to the cases where persistent bed-wetting leads to all-round family anxiety, concern and resentment. Simple causes such as infection (including worm infestation) and mental retardation need to be excluded and usually it emerges that the child is anxious and distressed, as are the parents. Reassurance all-round is called for. The majority stop around puberty. Active treatment may include the use of anti-depressants, such as Amitriptyline, whose Atropine-like side-effects delay bladder emptying or the use of conditioning methods, i.e. the pad and bell system where a bell is set off by wetting an electrical contact pad. The repetition of this experience causes the sufferer to awake if the bladder is sufficiently full. It should be remembered too that bed-wetting can run in families, e.g. a 38-year-old man became severely depressed and was treated with Amitriptyline in the days when its side-effects had not fully been appreciated. After 3 weeks he reported improvement but, above all, was delighted by the fact that he was now the only one of his adult four brothers who was dry at night. (A useful reminder too that nocturnal enuresis is more common in boys than in girls).

Encopresis

This is defined as persistent faecal soiling beyond age 2 years. The investigations and treatment look first of all towards simple causes such as cold, dank, dark and inaccessible lavatories as well as physiological rarities such as Hirschprung's disease.

Constipation may be caused by either of these, soiling occurs when the large bowel is overloaded and thus incontinent. Emotional factors are important. The child may have parents who are overfussy about regular bowel action as a sign of good health; or it may be found that their complaints of soiling are meaningless and based on their own overscrupulous obsessional concern with trivia. However, soiling does occur and may be related not only to over-rigid maternal insistence on child behaviour standards in all fields, but also to the fact that the child may have learnt to use soiling as the only way in which he can show aggression. At all events, the most useful treatment approach is to look carefully into the total picture and try to retrain the child's bowel habit in an atmosphere of calm and good sense. The parents will need to understand how to learn to behave in a way that converts bowel evacuation into a normal and civilized activity like washing the face or brushing the teeth, and then the child will learn to empty the bowel without fear of punishment for mistiming nor eager anticipation of praise for a socially acceptable lump of faeces. Above all, everyone needs to learn that human survival does not depend on the daily passage of a 'well-formed' stool and that there are considerable physiological variations in bowel habit. Some people defaecate once every 2 to 3 weeks and come

to no harm at all. The medical profession has created bowel hypochondriasis and must not be surprised if its earliest manifestations occur
in childhood.

ADOLESCENCE

Adolescent disturbances are more florid and more diverse. They come
nearer to adult disorders, but being coloured by the intensity of adolescent experience and development they often present in a more
dramatic and perplexing way. Social withdrawal is an important presenting symptom which may overlie disturbance ranging from fashionable
adolescent discontent to a serious psychosis such as schizophrenia or
the belated recognition of a syndrome such as autism, though the latter
is usually recognized before the age of 12 years. Autism is the classical
example of a psychiatric syndrome in that it is a term used to encompass
defective social and interpersonal relationships from early childhood,
speech disturbance and behaviour disturbance including impulsiveness,
overactivity, repetitive behaviour and seeming unawareness or indifference to the environment—human or mechanical. It has long been a
central issue in child psychiatry since the condition tended to be unrecognized, baffling and, worst of all, overlooked. The autistic child
tended to be included in the general categories of either psychosis or
subnormality and ended up as a long-term inmate of an institution.
Nowadays, at least there is growing awareness of the special needs of the
autistic child. The most important special needs are early recognition
and adequate training and education towards comprehensible communication and easier relationships. The aetiology is baffling though the
rubric of autism may well cover a wide range of recognizable disorders
varying from mental retardation to psychosis but always leaving a large
group of children over whom rest the question marks ?psychotic ?cause.
At least it can be said that child psychiatry has progressed far beyond the
point when it was assumed that autistic children were always the offspring of neglectful, disdainful, overintellectualized 'refrigerator
parents' who made their children autistic by lofty disregard. Present
knowledge suggests a continuum of causes from brain damage and
mental retardation to extreme parental rejection. Whatever may be the
most important aetiological factor, the barely concealed moralistic attitudes of psychiatrists and social workers, about the rightness and
wrongness of child-rearing methods, are never helpful.
    The withdrawn adolescent always causes widespread concern, start-

ing in the family and extending beyond it to school and/or job. This is possibly because in Western society people are expected to be outgoing, diverse in interest and activity and generally acceptable in the social group. Here we enter a delicate area since the varieties of acceptable social behaviour may easily be questioned. A surprising number of withdrawn adolescents turn out to have depressive syndromes. Depression is something that adolescents were supposed not to have: in fact they do. Often it is related to real stress—fear of failure, fear of not being regarded as acceptable by their peers. Anxiety and neurotic disorders including hypochondriasis and obsessional problems can also cause the adolescent to seem either withdrawn or 'difficult'.

Adolescence then is well recognized as a time of stress and turmoil. Pressures go beyond mere concern about appearance and ambition and extent into very real problems created by the natural and biologically healthy rebelliousness of adolescents where adult authoritarian views are challenged and examined, often with unnerving accuracy. At the present time, the 'teenager' is a highly exploited individual in financial and possibly other terms.

Apart from any doubts the adolescent may have about his own personal future, it does seem that adolescents are now under greater pressures than ever they have been before. Earlier reference was made to the near psychotic break-down which resembles schizophrenia called the adolescent crisis of identity. It cannot be too strongly reiterated that it is important to distinguish this from true schizophrenia.

No-one would quarrel with the source material for anxiety in adolescence. The problem is to investigate the symptom in a sensible way. In this way one should be able to avoid chronicity and the carry-over of unresolved problems into adult life. The depressed adolescent may present with mood disturbance. More commonly, he presents as a withdrawn apathetic youngster with suicidal feelings. Here it should be repeated that no suicidal remark, no matter how chance, lightly stated, nor seemingly trivial, should ever be ignored. The schizophrenic adolescent may show preoccupation with seemingly abstruse topics, may appear to be day dreaming and show odd eccentric behaviour. On the other hand, a perfectly normal adolescent may display all of these characteristics so that the investigation of apparent personality change in an adolescent is a crucial matter in psychiatric practice. The diagnosis of schizophrenia in adolescents is an important matter and the diagnosis must not be made lightly. The too generous diagnosis of schizophrenia in young people may lead to disaster. Being labelled schizophrenic mistakenly can cause a youngster to lose the chance of employment, marriage and a whole series of life experiences and the endpoint can be summarized in the word 'misery'. For some, indeed, it may be as effective as extermination and result in the individual's exclusion from the world of the acceptably sane. Nevertheless, the early recognition of schizophrenia in adolescents and the start of vigorous treatment with Phenothiazines should prevent deterioration into chronicity.

Another important syndrome in adolescence is that of school refusal. It may arise in early childhood from a variety of causes. These may be obvious, e.g. an uncongenial scholastic ambiance, playground bullies and fear of failure. It may also develop because the child is neurotic and insecure or because the parent is neurotic and overdependent and unable to part with an equally overdependent child. At its worst, the syndrome becomes one of school phobia where the child is overwhelmed by anxiety at the threat of parting. Truancy is another matter, consisting of a continuum of behaviour where truancy is normal, e.g. 'fine day' truancy to persistent truancy. This persistent truancy is one of the most important predictors of juvenile delinquency and later adult criminality. In all cases of school refusal an adequate assessment of the extent of the problem can only be made after the fullest examination of the school, the child, and the parental and social background.

Aggressive behaviour in adolescence ranges from the truculent protest of near normal development to the impulsive aggression of the schizophrenic or the wilful destructiveness of the child who already has an impaired and possibly badly damaged personality.

REFERENCES

Crisp A. H. (1967) Anorexia nervosa. *Br. J. Hosp. Med.*, 3, 713.
Critchley M. (1964) *Developmental Dyslexia.* Heinemann, London.
Hersov L. A. (1977) School refusal. In *Child Psychiatry: Modern Approaches* (Eds M. Rutter & L. A. Hersov). Blackwell Scientific Publications, Oxford.
Robins L. (1966) *Deviant Children Grown Up.* Williams and Wilkins, Baltimore.
Russell G.F.M. (1977) Editorial: the present status of anorexia nervosa. *Psychol. Med.* 7, 363.
Russell G. F. M. (1966) *Children of Sick Parents: An Environmental and Psychiatric Study.* Maudsley Monograph No. 16. Oxford University Press, Oxford.
Rutter M. L., Graham P., Chadwick O. & Yule W. (1976) Adolescent turmoil: fact or fiction? *J. Child Psychol. Psychiat.*, 17, 35.
Wing L. (1970) The syndrome of early childhood autism. *Br. J. Hosp. Med.*, 4, 381.

CHAPTER 10
PSYCHIATRIC DISORDERS IN
THE ELDERLY

Introduction

If youth and adolescence are times of emotional development, maturation and turbulence, so old age, is, psychologically speaking, a time of relative stability. However, this relative stability is often more apparent than real and it should be realized that old age often brings psychological difficulties. Quite apart from this the elderly person faces special physical and social problems.

Once an individual becomes old the physical aspects and hazards of ageing become apparent. His joints and skin lose their elasticity and he becomes prone to those common disorders of the heart and circulation which are such an important feature of the morbidity of the 60–70 age group. It is unfortunate that at this time in his life the average person usually undergoes a major social change, e.g. retirement or widowhood. There are, therefore, obvious sources of stress in old age which merit enumeration.

1 Increasing physical ill health, e.g. Hypertension, ichaemic heart disease, chronic bronchitis.
2 Poverty.
3 Loneliness.
4 Loss of a marital partner.
5 Altered social role in a competitive society.
6 Fear of death.
7 Malnutrition.

The particular psychological disadvantage of the old person is a lack of flexibility.

In old age personality traits are already well established and patterns of behaviour relatively fixed. It is a commonplace finding that rigidity of outlook and feeling are part of the normal manifestations of ageing.

It is, therefore, always important to bear this in mind when trying to assess the mental state of a supposedly abnormal elderly patient. A certain stubbornness and obstinacy which may be normal in the elderly person may be given undue value by a prejudiced or inexperienced observer.

Psychiatric syndromes in old age

From what has been stated above it will be clear that the special features of psychiatric syndromes in the elderly are related to the fact that the individual's personality is fixed, his capacity for change limited and hence, often, his reaction to a situation more calamitous than if he were 20 years younger.

AFFECTIVE DISORDERS

These are the most important group of illnesses to consider because the depressive states are so amenable to treatment.

It is, therefore, doubly important that the depressed elderly patient is not overlooked.

It is easy to mistake a state of chronic apathetic depression and suppose that an individual is a lonely old person when in fact he is a lonely depressed old person.

Classically the depressive illness of old age has been described as *involutional melancholia* but there is some controversy as to whether this is an illness peculiar to old age or merely the coincidence of the one with the other.

At all events the syndrome is notable for:
1 profound depressive affect,
2 striking degrees of agitation, and
3 massive ideas of guilt and self-recrimination, often of delusional intensity.

This variety of affective disorder is not difficult to diagnose. However, lesser degrees of depression may be.

One should, therefore, always be on the lookout for the apathy, hypochondriasis, inertia and sleep disturbance associated with depression.

Hypomanic excitement

In the elderly is not uncommon but is apt to be persistent and again may go unrecognized if not severe, e.g. an 86-year-old man, Mr S., was said to be presenting a difficult problem in management in a geriatric ward because of his interfering, restless behaviour. He was described as 'thieving and mischievous'. In fact on examination he presented a typical picture of mild hypomanic excitement with elation and some grandiose ideas. All this settled with appropriate medication.

Treatment

Antidepressant medication is the treatment of choice though severely depressed old people will respond very well to E.C.T. providing their physical conditions permit it.

Imipramine and Amitryptiline are the most frequently used anti-depressants in the elderly. Caution should be exercised in commencing these medications since the usual initial dose of 25 mg t.d.s. may induce states of excitement, or in the case of Amitryptiline, excessive drowsiness. It is therefore advisable to start off with 10 mg t.d.s.

PARANOID PSYCHOSES

Acute paranoid reactions are commonly encountered in the elderly. The patient may develop an acute illness in which agitation and persecutory notions are prominent. In many instances a strong *affective colouring* is found, whilst in others there may be evidence of *organic impairment.* Whatever the aetiology it is important to recognize that these acute disturbances, if handled carefully and sensibly, will have a good outcome.

The reaction may have been triggered off by some obvious event in the patient's life such as removal from home to an old people's home, or admission to hospital.

Such a change of environment may be too much for the old person who then becomes frightened, suspicious and bewildered, and if treated tactlessly, even by well-meaning individuals, may 'blow up' into a state of psychotic excitement.

Aetiology

Many paranoid syndromes in the elderly arise as an acute reaction set against a background of organic cerebral impairment. This is most commonly associated with either *cerebral arteriosclerosis* or *senile dementia.* Others are heavily coloured by affective symptoms and are probably *affective in origin.* They respond well to antidepressive treatment.

It should be remembered too that the old person *handicapped by deafness or blindness* is a likely candidate for a paranoid state.

Schizophrenic psychoses can arise in the elderly—these are little different in form from other schizophrenias. Finally the paranoid syndrome may be grafted on to a *lifelong paranoid personality disorder.*

ORGANIC SYNDROMES

Organic syndromes including subacute delirious states superimposed on dementia are commonplace in the elderly. It is not uncommon for such patients to require admission to hospital in an acutely disturbed state in which disorientation and restlessness are manifest.

Aetiology

A typical clinical picture is one of acute confusion with perplexity, restlessness, incoherence of thought and feeling. The most common setting for this is either *cerebral arteriosclerosis* or *SDAT* but in addition to this *acute confusional episodes in the elderly* can be caused by such events as myocardial infarction, bronchopneumonia, anaemia and uraemia. These four conditions should always be borne in mind. They are easily excluded and investigations aimed at this should be routine in the examination of the confused elderly person.

General considerations

Any elderly person who develops a psychiatric syndrome should be carefully evaluated in his or her home situation before the decision is taken to admit to a psychiatric hospital. Admission to hospital should only be arranged if there is a clear indication, i.e. if the patient can best be treated in hospital. It is vital that the elderly patient should not lose his or her place in the community. Whitehead has demonstrated convincingly the value of psychiatric admissions on a 'month in and month out' basis even with quite severly demented patients. In addition to this the elderly patient with psychiatric disturbance can be perfectly adequately maintained at day hospitals, or day centres.

The patient's physical health should be carefully investigated and disorders such as chronic bronchitis, ischaemic heart disease, prostatic enlargement, arthritis, etc., all searched for and given adequate treatment.

Of course, there are some patients who will require long-term care in mental hospital, e.g. those with severe states of dementia but these should be in the minority. Local authorities provide residential accommodation for patients with psycho-geriatric disturbance and these services should be utilized wherever possible.

Although in many instances the goals of psychiatric treatment in the elderly patient may be limited, the results are, none the less, often extremely gratifying. The dramatic relief of the depression previously unrecognized can cause such a radical alteration in the patient's way of life. Simple psychotherapy too is of great value. It is easy to avoid old people and all too often they are ignored and retreat into mildly hostile apathy. Simple discussion of their problems, acknowledgement of their status and awareness of their plight with sympathetic understanding can always produce considerable symptomatic relief.

REFERENCES

Allison R. S. (1962) *The Senile Brain: A Clinical Study*. Edward Arnold, London.

Lewis A. (1955) Mental aspects of ageing. Ciba Foundation Coll. *Ageing*, vol. 1, 32. Churchill, London.

Post F. (1962) *The Significance of Affective Symptoms in Old Age*. Maudsley Monographs 10, Oxford University Press, Oxford.

Post F. (1976) *Geriatric Depression*. (Eds Du Gallant & G. M. Simpson). Spectrum, New York.

Van Praag H. M. (1977) Psychotropic drugs in the aged. *Comp. Psychiat.*, **18**, 429.

Whitehead J. A. (1965) A comprehensive psycho-geriatric service. *Lancet*, **ii**, 583.

CHAPTER 11
PSYCHIATRY AND THE LAW
THE MENTAL HEALTH ACT, 1959
(Mental Health Amendment Bill, 1983)

Historical background

The history of the care of the mentally ill is on the whole a grim story consisting mainly of neglect, indifference and ill treatment, despite islands of progress. From time to time reforming persons halted this process and laws were passed to regulate the running of asylums for the insane and protect the inmates.

The main purpose of such institutions was custodial—if a patient entered, he stood only a small chance of returning to the world since little active treatment could be offered and society did not welcome his return, believing him to be dangerous and beyond hope of improvement.

The nineteenth century saw emphasis on the moral treatment of the insane, i.e. treating patients like human beings, and a great deal was accomplished to improve the care of patients, finding them useful occupations, removing restraint and encouraging a more hopeful attitude.

Nevertheless legislation was cumbersome, and even as late as 1890 the passage of the Lunacy Acts did not make the position easier. If anything the mental hospitals were fixed in a custodial role, since voluntary admission to mental hospital was impossible. A step forward occurred in 1930, with the Mental Treatment Act, which enabled people to enter hospital voluntarily. In the past 20 years, as knowledge and therapeutic zeal increased, it became apparent that a less unwieldy set of laws was needed. This culminated in 1959 with the Mental Health Act recently amended by the Mental Health Amendment Bill which came into effect on 30 September 1983 having received Royal Assent (October 1982).

The Mental Health Act 1959

This is a comprehensive act which repealed the Lunacy Acts of 1890 and the Mental Treatment Act of 1930. The most important general

112

features are as follows:

1 Control of mental hospitals and mental nursing homes etc., passes from the Board of Control to the National Health Service.

2 Informal admission of patients is encouraged.

3 The procedure surrounding compulsory admission to hospital is made more clinical and less formal and intimidating.

4 The role of the local authority in mental health services is defined.

The act is divided into nine parts:

Part 1 repeals previous legislation, defines and classifies mental disorder and proclaims informal admission	(Sec. 1–5)
Part 2 deals with the role of the local authority	(Sec. 6–13)
Part 3 deals with nursing homes etc.	(Sec. 14–24)
Part 4 deals with compulsory admission to hospital	(Sec. 25–59)
Part 5 deals with criminal patients	(Sec. 60–80)
Part 6 deals with special hospitals (for dangerous and violent patients)	(Sec. 97–99)
Part 8 deals with management of property and affairs of patients	(Sec. 100–121)
Part 9 Miscellaneous	(Sec. 122–124)

The sections of the Act of most interest to students are sections 25, 26, 29, and 30.

Section 25

Section 25 is used to detain a patient for a period not exceeding 28 days for purposes of observation. This is now being changed to 'admission for assessment for 28 days' the idea being that assessment will include treatment. Patients on such an order will have the right of appeal to a Mental Health Review Tribunal within 14 days of admission. A medical recommendation for admission is signed by two doctors:

1 the patient's own doctor (where possible), and

2 a doctor recognized by the Act as having special experience in psychiatry.

The application for admission is made by the nearest relative or if not available an approved social worker.

Section 26

As originally stated this was a section under which an order for treatment was made by two doctors, (one recognized as having special experience), on the grounds that the patient was a danger to himself or others and was unsuitable for informal admission. In the 1959 Act it was valid for 1 year. As amended now the order will last for 6 months. This is now true also for Section 60, a treatment order issued from a court by a judge on two medical recommendations.

Section 29

Provides a means of emergency admission. It permits the patient to be detained for 72 hours pending conversion to either S.25 or informal status.

The application is made by the nearest relative or approved social worker, and the medical recommendation is made by any registered practitioner providing he has seen the patient within 24 hours of signing.

Section 30

Provides for retention in hospital of a patient already in, who becomes ill and requires compulsory observation. This order, signed by the doctor in charge of the patient, authorizes his being kept in hospital for 3 days pending further action.

The other important provisions of the Mental Health Amendment Bill include:

1   A special health authority the 'Mental Health Act Commission' has been set up to set aside special safeguards for detained patients, i.e. those detained on Section 26. This provides for the giving of a second opinion for detained patients who are to be given treatment requiring the patient's consent and this will particularly apply where the patient is either unwilling or unable to consent. In such a case, a concurring second opinion will be required. Such treatments would include psycho-surgery and other specified treatments. In addition provision is made for treatments which require consent or second opinion and may include treatments such as medication and ECT and other forms of treatment specially defined.

2   Mental Welfare Officers will now be replaced by approved social workers who will have had special training and qualifications.

3   Holding power. Registered mental nurses will be enabled to detain an informal patient in hospital for 6 hours so that a doctor can give an opinion regarding the necessity for further detention.

4   The term mental subnormality is replaced by mental impairment and severe impairment. Mental impairment being defined as 'state of arrested incomplete development of mind which includes significant impairment of intelligence and social functioning and is associated with abnormally aggressive or serious irresponsible conduct'.

The Mental Health Act Commission will be an independent multi-disciplinary body which will in general exercise a protective and supervisory function regarding detained patients. With the object of preventing abuse of their rights and the imposition of treatment against their consent.

Criminal responsibility

It is an established principle of English law that a man is responsible for his own actions—that is to say that he intends their result. Therefore it follows that in the eyes of the law he must bear the responsibility for them. In the case of serious offences, responsibility is the more likely to be questioned. In the case of an individual suffering from mental illness committing a crime, it has been for many years argued that the man's state of mind must impair his responsibility for his acts. This has, however, not been easy to establish in a court of law since the law assumes everyone is sane, and insanity has to be proven. Since 1843 the courts have used the MacNaughten Rules as a test of insanity. These rules arose following the trial for murder of Daniel MacNaughten who killed Sir Robert Peel's private secretary. MacNaughten had paranoid delusions and was acquitted on the direction of the judge.

Subsequently judges formulated the rules as they have been known ever since, as a series of answers to questions put to them by the House of Lords. In practice the rules seek the answers to the questions:
1   Regarding the offence, did the accused know the nature and quality of the act?
2   If he did, did he know he was doing wrong?
3   If he knew the nature and quality of the act, was he labouring under a delusion?

Despite their apparent simplicity, the rules can be difficult to apply and make for only a limited acknowledgement of impaired responsibility. For years they have been the subject of controversy, both here and and in the U.S.A. Nevertheless they are still widely applied as tests of insanity in capital cases.

Since the Homicide Act of 1959 the Law in England and Wales has acknowledged the concept of diminished responsibility, which can be invoked if an accused person is shown to be suffering from 'such abnormality of mind ... as substantially to impair his responsibility'. The concept of diminished responsibility has not been accepted without reserve, and it has been pointed out that once allowance is made for diminished responsibility one is calling into question the whole idea of criminal responsibility at any level. A question that remains unresolved.

Testamentary capacity

The ability to make a valid will depends on the possession of 'sound disposing mind'. This is not defined in law but the concept is derived from the notion that the person concerned should fulfill the following criteria: he should understand the implications of the act of making a will, have a good idea of the extent of the estate and know who are the likely beneficiaries. Mental illness, whether through psychosis or organic cerebral disease, does not automatically debar someone from making a valid will, since even in chronic schizophrenia and in dementia there are often well-preserved areas of lucidity and contact with reality. A doctor should never witness a will irrespective of whether or not he is a beneficiary.

REFERENCES

Glueck S. (1963) *Psychiatry and the Law.* Tavistock, London.
Slater E. (1954) The MacNaughton rules and modern concepts of responsibility. *Br. med. J.*, ii, 713.
West D. J. (1982) Delinquency: Its roots, Careers and Prospects. In *Cambridge Studies in Criminology* (Ed. L. Radzinowiz) Heinemann, London.

CHAPTER 12
TREATMENT IN PSYCHIATRY

Introduction

The term 'Treatment' is used in a wide sense in psychiatry; specific remedies for illnesses of known aetiology are practically unknown, so treatment tends to be empirical and eclectic. Treatment therefore includes any measures used: (a) to influence the patient's mental state, and (b) to assist in his rehabilitation and return to the community.

The measures used comprise the following groups:

1 psychological	psychotherapy behaviour therapy	used to deal with individual's symptoms, illness and and personality
2 physical	pharmacologic agents e.g. sedatives tranquillizers antidepressant drugs	used in acute psychoses, depressive illness and 'maintenance' treatment of chronic illness
3 occupational	occupational therapy industrial therapy	used to divert, stimulate, entertain and encourage the patient's activity and interest plays an important part in rehabilitation by giving the patient the chance to work and earn in a sheltered environment

Certain measures may be of most value in the acute illness, e.g. physical treatment; others may be of most value in rehabilitation, e.g. industrial therapy. Patients should receive help in as many ways as possible. The acute illness may be controlled by tranquillizers which restore the patient's contact with reality and enable him to participate more successfully in psychotherapy, and derive some benefit from a therapeutic environment. Providing the environment is permissive and friendly, it is therapeutic rather than antitherapeutic. Social forces too, are important in colouring illness and adding features which are neither symptoms or signs of illness but merely behaviour patterns imposed by the environment. Violent behaviour has become less common since this was realized. The struggling patient brought into hospital and hurled into a padded room, isolated in total darkness, would be less than normal if he did not react in hostile fashion towards his surroundings.

It is important to realize that any hospital admission provokes anxiety mainly because of the uncertainty that the patient experiences and also because he feels his individuality threatened right from the beginning by simple things like having to undress and get into bed. After this, much that goes on in hospital seems to reinforce the feeling of isolation and lack of identity so that if the atmosphere is worsened by heightened uncertainty, tension and suppressed violence—all of which can be commonplace in a badly run psychiatric ward—one soon has all the ingredients for a situation of the sort which Kafka has described in such frightening fashion.

Future planning of district psychiatric services in England and Wales should help considerably towards finally removing the stigma and general unease that surround mental hospital admission. The psychiatric unit in a general hospital, working in close cooperation with local services, should provide the best way to use hospital admission without damaging the patient.

PSYCHOLOGICAL TREATMENT

Individual psychotherapy

Psychotherapy is treatment based on verbal communication between patient and doctor and the formation of a therapeutic relationship between them.

The simplest form, and the most widely practised is *supportive psychotherapy*, in which the patient is encouraged to talk freely about himself and his symptoms and problems without exploring his unconscious mental life. No attempt is made to give the patient insight about the possible origins of his difficulties. His defences are shored up rather than broken down.

Psychoanalysis is the most important type of analytic psychotherapy. The term 'psychoanalysis' is used in two main ways, first it refers to a form of psychotherapy, and secondly it gives the name to the school of psychology founded by S. Freud.

Psychoanalytic theory is a theory of personality structure and development which stresses the fundamental importance of childhood experience in forming the personality. Freud based his theory on observations made on patients he had treated. Classical Freudian theory has been modified by his followers but the central hypothesis is that human behaviour is determined predominantly by unconscious forces and motives springing from primitive emotional needs.

In psychoanalysis the analyst seeks to explore and modify the personality structure of the patient by intensive and prolonged exploration of this unconscious mental life. This is achieved by use of the technique of *free association*. The patient lies on a couch and allows his thoughts to wander in any direction—in this way dredging up unconscious material of which he has previously apparently been quite unaware. The reason for getting the patient to lie down is so as to cut down to a minimum visual stimuli which might distract. The analyst interprets to the patient the symbolic meaning of his dreams and fantasies, in this way helping him towards insight about himself. It is necessarily a prolonged and time-consuming process.

Analytic psychotherapy short of full-scale psychoanalysis, is commoner and less cumbersome a process, and tends to be concerned with more clearly defined goals such as:
1 resolution of conflict,
2 working through problems and viewing them in a different light,
3 the relief of pent-up feelings.

The relationship between doctor and patient in psychotherapy is of paramount importance. Much of the content of interviews is so to speak 'hot material' and the patient soon invests the therapist with a good deal of feeling. Feelings of dependence, love, affection and hostility are common and the therapist has to know how to handle them and how to interpret their meaning to the patient. A personal analysis provides the only training for the psychoanalyst.

A non-analytic psychotherapist gains a great deal from a personal analysis but if this is not possible the good psychotherapist needs to be intelligent, intuitive, patient and above all, flexible.

Individual psychotherapy does not end with psychoanalysis. In fact psychoanalysis is probably the least commonly practised form of psychotherapy since it is time-consuming and uneconomical. On the other hand most psychotherapies owe a good deal to psychoanalytic theory without acknowledging it. In recent years there has been a move away from the 'classical' psychoanalytic type therapy towards briefer psychotherapies. Some concentrate on the meaning of the symptom, i.e. 'what sort of help is this patient *really* asking for?' Others pay particular attention to the 'here and now' situation, moving the patient all the time towards solving a particular problem in his life that he appears to be avoiding. While other psychotherapies are directed at the patient in a way that does not seem explicit but which moves the patient towards independence and self-reliance. Other psychotherapies are existential not only in following existential philosophy, but also in practical terms in that they encourage the patient towards responsibility for the self and one's actions, at the same time helping the patient to look at himself as a person in the world and to achieve some understanding of the meaning and significance of his existence.

Group psychotherapy

In group therapy the main focus of interest is on the inter-relationships within the group, rather than on the highly personal relationships as in individual therapy. Problems are shared in the group situation, and patients are able to see their own difficulties in interpersonal relation-ships reflected in the group, and so in a different light. Also they are subject to criticism, encouragement and support from other members of the group.

In practice groups should be small—about twelve members being the ideal number. It is found useful to select members of similar ages and with equal division of sexes. The therapist sits with the group—topics are discussed freely, the therapist adopts a non-directive role, avoiding domination or direction of the group but preventing them from straying into defensive irrelevancies.

Abreaction

Is the name given to a therapeutic process in which a patient relives an important past experience which has contributed significantly to the development of his illness. The re-enactment is accompanied by dis-charge of pent-up feeling. Freud found this happening to his patients, particularly under hypnosis, and he reasoned that it would be valuable to induce such states so that the patient would benefit by the emotional discharge. The technique of abreaction is used mainly in acute conversion hysteria precipitated by traumatic events, e.g. wartime disasters. Various methods other than hypnosis have been used to bring about a state of altered consciousness conducive to abreaction. The most widely used is the slow intravenous injection of a 5% solution of sodium amytal.

Behaviour therapy

Is the general name given to a relatively recent form of psychological treatment. Behaviour therapy has its roots in behaviouristic psychology as opposed to psychotherapy which is founded on dynamic psychology.

Behaviouristic psychology explains human behaviour in terms of stimulus—response mechanisms. Behaviour is regarded as learnt by Pavlovian conditioning processes governed by such processes or drive reduction. Thus neurotic behaviour is simply explained in terms of maladaptive behaviour rather than being linked with complicated intrapersonal, emotional development.

It follows from this view of neurotic illness that if the neurotic symptom is removed, the illness disappears too—an entirely opposite view to the psychodynamic one which sees symptoms as symbolic representations of internal conflict. A behaviouristic explanation of a phobic anxiety state would be that the patient has become conditioned to experience anxiety whenever he perceives certain signals and that this conditioned response has gradually generalized so that it is triggered off by a wide variety of signals.

Behaviour therapy seeks to eradicate the maladaptive response by a process of desensitization. Wolpe has pointed out that the anxiety response can be inhibited by placing the individual in situations resembling those which provoke anxiety, but which are sufficiently unlike them not to trigger off any anxiety. This builds up a generalizing process of reciprocal inhibition of anxiety, which is reinforced by rewards in the form of further anxiety-free situations.

Cognitive behaviour therapy

This is a relatively new development in behaviour therapy in which the basic assumption is that an individual's patterns of thinking influence behaviour and feeling and thus, by a series of rationally determined procedures, it should be possible to alter abnormal behaviours and feelings. It has found its widest expression to date in the treatment of depressive states.

PHYSICAL TREATMENT

Nowhere is empiricism more evident than in the sphere of physical treatment in psychiatry. Methods have appeared; a remarkable array of drugs is on the market; all are greeted with initial uncritical enthusiasm and later more soberly evaluated. The whole question of the use of physical treatments has aroused strong feelings on both sides. Nevertheless it is a fact that certain physical treatments have established themselves as important therapies which have revolutionized psychiatry.

Psychotropic drugs

Psychotropic drugs are special in that they alter feeling, perception and behaviour without significantly altering consciousness. The study of such drugs, i.e. psychopharmacology, has not only produced a large range of drugs used in treatment but has also suggested possible lines of research in the biochemistry of mental illness. The *cerebral amine* theory of depression is a good example. According to this theory the central transmitting amines are linked to depression in that it appears that depression can be associated with a low concentration of amines and mania with excessive concentrations. The amines concerned are Noradrenaline, 5-Hydroxy tryptamine (5-HTT or serotonin) and dopamine. The tricyclic antidepressants are thought to act by blocking the reabsorption of free amines and the monoamine oxidase inhibitors to act by preventing oxidative deamination, i.e. in either case causing higher amine concentrations.

The important psychotropic drugs include: Neuroleptics (major tranquillizers); antidepressants; tranquillizers (anxiolytic drugs); lithium.

1   Neuroleptics and tranquillizers

Tranquillizers are drugs which alter behaviour without impairing consciousness. Their place in psychiatry dates from 1953 when the tranquillizing effects of *Chlorpromazine* were first demonstrated. *Chlorpromazine* was the first of the phenothiazines to come into use, and the majority of the tranquillizers in present use belong to the phenothiazine series. Phenothiazines all have the basic structure:

Where R1 and/or R2 are side chains varying from one phenothiazine to another.

Chlorpromazine (Largactil) is most useful in calming psychotic excitement whether organic, affective or schizophrenic in origin. It is widely used in the maintenance treatment of chronic psychotic patients, but the usefulness here is much less certain. It can be administered by either the intramuscular or oral route. *Dosage* is up to a maximum of 600 mg per day in divided doses, though a maximum of 400 mg per day is rarely exceeded.

The most serious *side-effects* include anaemia, agranulocytosis and jaundice. Less important effects include hypotensive attacks, photo-sensitivity and dermatitis.

Chlorpromazine potentiates the action of barbiturates, alcohol, anaesthetics and narcotic drugs.

Promazine (Sparine) is a phenothiazine of similar structure and action though probably less powerful, weight for weight, than chlorpromazine. Side-effects such as rashes and hypotension may be less than with chlorpromazine.

Thioridazine (Melleril) has a similar dosage range to chlorpromazine, and similar actions.

Trifluoperazine (Stelazine) is an important drug of the prochlor-perazine series (derived from the phenothiazines). It is said to have an alerting and antihallucinogenic effect in contrast to the sedative effect of the other phenothiazines. It is widely used in the treatment of both acute and chronic schizophrenic patients. It can be administered parenterally or orally. *Dosage* ranges from 5–40 mg per day in divided doses. There is evidence to suggest that in small doses (3 mg t.d.s.) it is useful in the treatment of chronic anxiety states.

Long acting phenothiazine drugs. The most effective long acting pheno-thiazine drug in present use is fluphenazine decanoate (Modecate). This has replaced its precursor fluphenazine enanthate. The decanoate variant is a long acting phenothiazine drug which is injected by deep intramuscular injection and its duration of action is 1 month. The advantage of this drug is that it removes the problems associated with the patient who is unwilling or who forgets to take medication regularly. Extrapyramidal side-effects do occur and can produce severe dystronic reactions. A common practice is to give anti-parkinsonian medication by injection at the same time as the decanoate. Common practice consists in giving the patient a first test dose of 12.5 mg of the decanoate and then following it up with the 25 mg monthly dose. There is no evidence to show that increasing the dose beyond 25 mg a month has any appreciable effect on schizophrenic psychoses. One important side-effect that is noted in the use of decanoate is depression.

Side-effects of phenothiazines

These are most commonly neurological syndromes affecting extra-pyramidal system, they include:
1 Motor restlessness particularly affecting the legs (akathisia).
2 Facial rigidity   ⎫ Parkinsonian
3 Increased tonus in all four limbs ⎬ syndrome.
4 Persistent tongue protrusion and involuntary mouth movements.
5 Dystonic movements of the head and neck.
These side-effects can be controlled by using anti-parkinsonian drugs, which should however not be given as a routine. Patients who have been on long-term phenothiazine therapy may develop the syndrome of Tardive Dyskinesia. This consists of persistent facial movements, grimacing and tongue protrusion which do not stop if the medication is discontinued.

2   Antidepressant drugs

Drugs used in the treatment of depression fall into two main groups: (a) the tricyclic series, and (b) the monoamine oxidase inhibitors.

The first drugs used in the treatment of depression were *amphetamine and its derivatives*. They had the advantage of cheapness and a lack of minor side-effects. Unfortunately the dangers of abuse and addiction have made their use undesirable. Also they are not effective in severe depression.

The tricyclic series

Table 1 lists the most commonly used tricyclic antidepressants. It appears that tricyclic antidepressants act in various ways; some by inhibiting the reabsorption of Serotonin (Amitriptyline, Imipramine, Clomipramine), while others inhibit the reabsorption of noradrenaline (Desipramine, Protriptyline and Nortriptyline).

Dosage: It is now realized that the half-life of tricyclic antidepressant is such that there is no need to use divided daily doses. Common practice now is to give a once daily dosage at night.

Table 1

Generic name	Trade name	Daily dose (mg)	Comment
Imipramine	Tofranil	75–200	The first and, to date, the most effective.
Nortriptyline	Aventyl	75–150	Mildly stimulant.
Protriptyline	Concordin	15–45	Mildly stimulant. Higher risk of tachycardia and cardiac arrhythmias.
Iprindole	Prondol	45–90	Mildly stimulant.
Amitriptyline	Tryptizol	75–200	Sedative—hence often given in one dose at night.
Trimipramine	Surmontil	75–150	Sedative—hence often given in one dose at night.
Doxepin	Sinequan	75–150	Sedative, marked anxiolytic action.
Dothiepin	Prothiaden	75–150	Sedative.
Clomipramine	Anafranil	75–100	Sedative. Bad interaction with alcohol.

Side-effects of tricyclic antidepressants

A wide range have been reported, the more common varieties are listed:
1 Cardiovascular: hypertension, *orthostatic hypotension*, palpitations, *tachycardia*, arrhythmias.
2 Anticholinergic: *Dry mouth*, nausea and vomiting, *constipation*, urinary delay and retention, difficulty in accommodation, mydriasis, *blurred vision*, sublingual adenitis, sweating.
3 Central nervous system: confusional states, excitement, agitation and restlessness, *insomnia*, paraesthesia and tingling, ataxia, tremor, fits.
4 Skin: general and non-specific; rashes, photosensitivity, urticaria, oedema—especially of tongue and face.
   Non-specific side-effects include impotence, *drowsiness*, feelings of *weakness and fatigue*, *weight gain*, weight loss.
5 Rarer adverse effects include myocardial infarction, heart block, extrapyramidal side-effects, paralytic ileus, depression of bone marrow activity, agranulocytosis, purpura, thrombocytopenia, black tongue,

gynaecomastia and testicular swelling, breast enlargement and galactorrhoea, alopecia.

Comment. Tricyclic antidepressants are very widely prescribed and it is for question now as to whether they are being overprescribed. The incidence of side-effects is high and also there is a dangerous level of mortality from cardiac arrest and arrhythmia, either with overdose in cases of overdose and sometimes in cases of therapeutic dosage. For this reason, caution should be used in their use and the time really has arrived when the whole question of the widespread use of tricyclic antidepressant drugs needs seriously to be reconsidered since it is beyond doubt that many people who are not depressed are given these drugs and so exposed to considerable hazard. Not every unhappy person who consults a doctor is necessarily depressed.

The monoamine oxidase inhibitors

The first demonstration of the euphoriant effect of this group of drugs was that INAH used in the treatment of tuberculosis made patients euphoric. Since then a large number of MAO inhibitors have been developed. Probably the most common in use are: Isocarboxazid (Marplan) Dosage range 15–30 mg t.d.s.; Phenelzine (Nardil) Dosage range 15–30 mg t.d.s.; Tranylcypromine (Parnate) Dosage range 15 mg t.d.s. to 15 mg q.d.s.

Side-effects of monoamine oxidase inhibitors

1   Potentiation of barbiturates, alcohol, tranquillizers, opiates and Pethidine. For this reason their use presents special hazards in anaesthesia.
2   States of excitement and agitation.
3   Hypotension.
4   Hypertensive crises. These occur in certain patients if they eat foods containing *tyramine* such as certain cheeses, yeast extracts and broad bean pods. Patients should be warned not to eat these foods. The crises when they occur are characterized by severe headache which can simulate subarachnoid haemorrhage.
5   Liver damage. This has been found most commonly in the Hydrazine series (phenelzine, isocarboxazid).
6   Other common side-effects include oedema, sexual impotence and failure of orgasm; also dryness of the mouth, blurred vision and constipation.

Combinations of MAO inhibitors and tricyclic antidepressants can be dangerous and are probably best avoided or left to the expert.

General observations on the use of antidepressant drugs

Though they are widely prescribed, there is by no means universal agreement either as to their efficacy or mode of action. Controlled trials have revealed conflicting results. On the one hand there are those workers who are convinced that antidepressant drugs exert a specific effect on the supposed depressive process, whilst on the other there are those who claim that the drugs act merely by their sedative effect on agitation and anxiety. It has been pointed out that depression has a high rate of natural remission and that the enthusiasm for effects of anti-depressant drugs may be accounted for by this alone. Whatever the facts may turn out to be, one thing seems certain and that is that physicians have become more alerted to depression and its existence as a condition meriting attention and treatment.

3 Drugs used in the treatment of anxiety

Tranquillizers have now completely replaced barbiturates and they include:
1 Chlordiazepoxide (Librium) 10–40 mg t.d.s.
2 Diazepam (Valium) 10–40 mg t.d.s.
3 Lorazepam (Ativan) 0.5–2 mg t.i.d.
4 Oxazepam (Serenid) 10–30 mg t.d.s.

The newest group of drugs used in the treatment of anxiety are the beta-adrenergic receptor blocking agents of which the most commonly used is propanolol hydrochloride (Inderal), dosage 80–160 mg daily. Beta blocking agents should not be used if there is a history of asthma, in metabolic acidosis, after prolonged fasting or in the presence of 2nd and 3rd degree heart block. In general propanolol is well tolerated but mild side-effects include cold hands and feet, nausea, insomnia, lassitude and diarrhoea. These can usually be offset by building up the dose gradually. Isolated cases of purpura and paraesthesia of the hands has been reported. If bradycardia or hypotension occur, the drug should be withdrawn. In general we can say that the beta blocking drugs are being much more widely used with patients with somatic manifestations of anxiety, i.e. tremor, palpitations, sweating and general feeling of tension.

Vitamins

Large doses of vitamins of the B group are used routinely: (a) in the treatment of delirium tremens; and (b) in the treatment of subacute delirious states.

Electro-convulsive therapy

Of all physical treatments E.C.T. is apparently the most successful, yet its mode of action is unknown and in some quarters its use is viewed with suspicion. Speculative theories of a neurophysiologic sort suggest that the convulsion alters the conditionability of an intricate system or that in some way it alters the level of arousal of the central nervous system. Other theorists suggest that in some unknown way it alters the balance of a central mood regulating mechanism. These tend to represent the views of those favouring its use.

Those who are on the whole opposed to its use tend to suggest that it is a form of 'shock' treatment which in a way 'shocks' the patient into altered behaviour as in the past patients were 'shocked' by sudden immersion or being whirled around in revolving chairs. It has also been suggested that it is the sudden loss of consciousness which affects the patient. Nevertheless there is more uniformity of agreement about its usefulness than is the case with drugs.

Origins

It was first used in 1938 by Cerletti and Bini. It had previously been incorrectly supposed that there was a negative correlation between epilepsy and schizophrenia and on the basis of this it was suggested that schizophrenia might be treated by convulsions. Meduna started by using chemically induced convulsions in 1935, while Cerletti and Bini were the first to use electrically induced fits.

The results in treating depression were soon shown to be successful. Depressive mood and agitation were replaced by normal mood within days of starting treatment, and it is in the treatment of depression that E.C.T. has an established place. It is successful in approximately 85% of cases of depression. Whether or not it prevents recurrences is questionable but it does shorten the illness.

Its place in the treatment of schizophrenia is controversial, though most experienced workers suggest that it should always be tried. Acute schizophrenic episodes and schizoaffective illnesses respond best to it.

Technique

A typical machine gives a 100 V discharge for 1 second. This induces instant loss of consciousness followed by convulsion. Nowadays it is usual to give modified E.C.T. and the practice is to modify it by using intravenous anaesthesia (Thiopentone 200–250 mg in a 5% solution) with a muscle relaxant (Scoline or Brevidil) to prevent injury by violent muscular contractions. Oxygen is used to ventilate the patient, and the convulsion is induced. Recovery of consciousness is rapid, e.g. within 10 minutes, and discomfort is no more than a pin prick in the arm. Atropine 1/75 gr is given intravenously with the Thiopentone.

Treatment is given twice weekly and the patient assessed between treatments. A course of treatment is not prescribed; it is preferable to stop when the patient is better. One should rarely give more than twelve treatments.

Hazards of E.C.T.

These are:
Major
1   Normal anaesthetic hazards.
2   Special cardiovascular hazard, e.g. induction of cardiac arrhythmia.
3   Injury to tongue, teeth, bones (longbones, scapula, crush fractures of vertebral bodies).
Minor
4   Amenorrhea.
5   Headache.
6   Burns.
7   Memory loss.
8   Confusional states.

Psycho-surgery

Psycho-surgery is now much less extensively practised. The original rather crude types of leucotomy operation have been replaced by highly modified and restricted surgery aimed at dividing connections between the frontal lobes and the thalamus. Other operations such as cingulectomy have also been used. These types of surgery show the best results when persistent tension is present particularly if it arises on the basis of a depressive state or in obsessional disorders and rarely in chronic schizophrenia. Surgery, though less widely performed still has a place in carefully selected cases for the relief of chronic states of tension.

OCCUPATIONAL

Occupational therapy

For many years it has been realized that work can be a source of diversion to the disturbed patient. Nowadays the occupational therapist has a wide range of activities to offer the psychiatric patient. These include art and craft work which can calm the anxious patient or revive the interest of the retarded depressive. Tasks can be provided for the brain-damaged patient which may afford him some degree of satisfaction.

Also the occupational therapist can assess the limits of such a patient's ability and help to provide him with a suitable environment. In rehabilitation the O.T. department can help to plan a patient's daily round of activity to prepare for the return home by helping him to acquire new skills or refurbish old ones. The housewife can be particularly helped in this direction by the provision of a kitchen unit in the O.T. department. Ideally occupational therapy should be realistic and diverse and as far removed as possible from the traditional picture of basket making or the manufacture of useless ornaments.

Industrial therapy

This is an attempt to provide the patient with a working day, a regular wage and the prospects of working outside hospital.

It provides a sheltered working environment for the chronic patient where he can learn, practise and gain confidence in new skills.

In many hospitals light assembly work etc. is done on a contract basis with local firms and after a patient has 'proved himself', he can then go out to work.

Rehabilitation of chronic patients, particularly chronic schizophrenics, is a difficult task. Patients need graded tasks, much encouragement, careful assessment and supervision. In this the doctor is aided by many people including:
1   nurses with special training and experience,
2   social workers,
3   psychologists, and
4   disablement resettlement officers.

SOCIAL MEASURES

The social worker

The social worker occupies a central place in psychiatric practice bringing to it not only a knowledge of social factors and their importance in the aetiology of illness but also more sophisticated awareness of psychodynamics than that possessed by the non-psychiatric social worker. This is not to suggest that the social worker should be some form of psychotherapist manqué since this would mean too limited a function. The work of the social worker includes such diverse activities as:

1   collection of data,
2   highlighting of areas of social relevance in a patient's life situation,
3   direct counselling about concrete social problems such as finance, housing, etc.,
4   social casework: this is a therapeutic technique in which the social worker helps the patient to handle his problems, and relate them to his social situation,
5   helping a patient to get psychiatric advice,
6   prophylaxis of psychiatric disorder,
7   group discussions with the spouses of patients who have a common problem (e.g. alcoholics' wives),
8   after care and follow up.

The therapeutic community

All hospitals are frightening places for the majority of patients, and mental hospitals are particularly so, since often they tend to be large, gaunt buildings with long anonymous corridors. In fact if one were to try and devise a way of making a patient worse one could hardly improve on traditional mental hospital custodial care, which tended to reduce patients to nameless lost creatures, with no identity. In fairness to those who worked in such conditions it should be pointed out that they did not have the advantages of the tranquillizing drugs of today nor enthusiastic support except from a few. It is also incorrect to suppose that 'open door' policies are a twentieth-century phenomenon. They are really an extension of the best of English nineteenth-century psychiatry. Unfortunately, as is often the case, pioneering ideas were forgotten and had to be rediscovered.

The moment anyone enters *any* hospital an attack is made on his existence as an individual—his clothes are removed and he is put to bed and he becomes another patient. In general hospitals, this matters less since the duration of stay is short and the experience is soon forgotten. But for the psychiatric patient it can be disastrous, since he may be entering hospital for a long stay. Before the importance of social factors in influencing mental illness was generally appreciated, the object was to make the patient conform to a number of arbitrary behavioural standards often of a fairly absurd sort, as quickly as possible. Authority was hierarchical and not to be defied. This made tension increase and violence the more likely.

Patients soon learnt to survive by adapting themselves to numbed acquiescence with consequent loss of initiative and drive, so called 'institutional neurosis'. This was aided by isolation from visitors and lack of activity.

Belatedly it has been realized that the community in which the patient lives can have either a therapeutic or an antitherapeutic effect and attempts are now made to produce a hospital environment which preserves the patient's individuality and stimulates him to activity and a return to the world outside.

Emphasis is laid on freeing the lines of communication between medical and nursing staff and encouraging free discussion between patients and staff, thus removing artificial and meaningless barriers. Of course running hospitals in this way means more work and more trouble as opposed to the apparent calm of a traditional 'well run' hospital supervised by a superintendent delegating authority downwards. It means more work, but less misery and more hope. Psychiatric patients need hope, noise, colour and activity. Too often their lives can be spent in a grey silence. Anyone who can prevent this is performing a therapeutic act.

REFERENCES

Eysenck H. J. (1960) *Behaviour Therapy and the Neuroses.* Pergamon Press, London.
Finesinger J. E. (1948) Psychiatric interviewing. *Am. J. Psychiatry,* 105, 187.
Hordern A. & Hamilton M. (1963) Drugs and moral treatment. *Br. J. Psychiatry,* 109, 500.
May A. R. (1961) Prescribing community care for the mentally ill. *Lancet,* i, 760.
Rapaport R. N. (1960) *Community as Doctor.* Tavistock, London.
Rees W. L. (1966) Drugs used in the treatment of psychiatric disorders. *Abstr. Wld. Medicine,* 39, 129.

Scull A. (1981) *Madhouses, Mad-Doctors and Madmen. The Social History of Psychiatry in the Victorian Era.* University of Pennsylvania Press, Philadelphia.

Stanton A. H. & Schwartz M. S. (1954) *The Mental Hospital.* Basic Books, New York.

Shepherd M., Lader M. & Rodnight R. (1968) *Clinical Psychopharmacology.* English University Press, London.

Tooth G. C. & Brook E. M. (1961) Trends in the mental hospital population and their effect on future planning. *Lancet,* i, 710.

Weissmann N. M. (1976) Psychotherapy and behaviour therapy. *Lancet,* ii, 45.

Wolpe J. (1958) *Psychotherapy by Reciprocal Inhibition.* Stanford University Press, California.

INDEX

Childbirth, depression 19
Childhood, psychiatric disorders
    101–4
Chlordiazepoxide (Librium) 59, 67,
    127
  in alcoholism 77
  in delirium tremens 76
Chlormethiazole (Hemineverin)
  in alcoholism 77
  in delirium tremens 76
Chlorpromazine (Largactil) 122–3
  in alcoholism 77
  in schizophrenia 39
Chromosome abnormalities 92,
    94–6
Cingulotomy 129
Cocaine, dependence 82
Cognition, testing 11–12
Commonsense, and intelligence 91
Compulsive disorders *see* Obsessional
    disorders
Concentration testing 12
Conditioned avoidance 61
Confabulation 49, 76
Confusion, in elderly 110
Constipation, encopresis and 103
Constitutional neuroticism 57
Conversion hysteria 62–3
  treatment 64–5, 121
Cri du chat 95
Criminal responsibility 115–16
Cyclothymia 25

Deconditioning, in phobias 57, 60
Delirium 43–5
  clinical manifestations 43–5
  definition 6
  diagnosis 45
  treatment 48
Delirium tremens 49, 76, 128
Delusional ideas 6, 26
Delusions 10–11
  definition 6
  schizophrenic 34–5
Dementia 43, 45–6
  aetiology 46–7
  alcoholic 76

clinical manifestations 45–6
definition 5
emotional changes 46
multi-infarct 49
praecox *see* Schizophrenia
pre-senile 51
traumatic 50
treatment 48
Depersonalization, definition 6
Depression 16–24
  adolescent 105
  aetiology 17–20
  associated disorders 20–2
  cerebral amine theory 122
  complications 22–3
  definition 5
  differential diagnosis 22
  endogenous 16
  heredity 17
  incidence and prevalence 17
  physiological precipitators 19
  prognosis 25
  reactive 15–16
  sex ratio 18
  social aspects 18, 19
  treatment 23–4, 124–7
  see also Manic-depressive disorders
Derealization, definition 6
Desensitization *see* Deconditioning
Diazepam (Valium) 59, 67, 127
  dependence 80
  in alcoholism 77
Diminished responsibility concept
    116
Distress 1
Disturbed children 100
Disulfiram (Antabuse), in alcoholism
    77
Doctor-patient relationship 2
Dopamine hypothesis, schizophrenia
    32
Double bind theory, schizophrenia
    31
Down's syndrome (mongolism) 92,
    94
Drinking behaviour, modification
    78
Drug-using behaviour 81